Hors-d'oeuvres

Hors-d'oeuvres

Carla Homan & Joyce Palmer

Hurtig Publishers
Edmonton

Hurtig Publishers Ltd.
10560−105 Street
Edmonton, Alberta
Canada   T5H 2W7

Canadian Cataloguing in Publication Data

Homan, Carla, 1951-
  Hors-d'oeuvres

  Includes index.
  ISBN 0-88830-268-1

  1. Cookery (Appetizers)   I. Palmer,
Joyce, 1932-   II. Title.
TX740.H64 1984   641.8'12   C84-091288-9

To Harry & Menno

Design: David Shaw & Associates Ltd.
Photography: Peter Duthie
Illustration: Dzidra Mitchell

Printed and bound in Canada
by D. W. Friesen & Sons Limited

Contents

Introduction/7
Dips & Spreads/10
Fillings for Pastries, Vegetables & Sandwiches/27
Pastry/36
Fish, Meat & Poultry/63
Home-Made Condiments/80
Sweet Indulgence/87
Punches & Coolers/94
''The Nuts''/100
Menu Suggestions/103
Metric Conversions/108
Index/109

Introduction

Here is a collection of our favourite hors-d'oeuvre recipes —one result of an ongoing partnership based on a mutual love of cooking, entertaining & (we must confess) eating!

Having met briefly in Toronto in 1974 our friendship really began in 1976 when we were reunited in Calgary. Our first joint venture found us on the tennis court, but our over-the-net confessions soon led to the discovery that our true common ground was a love of cooking. Joyce, a devoted student of cookbooks & cooking magazines, had long been a food hobbyist, experimenting with a variety of cuisines. As a high school student Carla had catered wedding showers & cocktail parties, thanks to her mother's patience & a large fridge. We found too that a dash of the entrepreneur simmered in us both.

So we began as caterers for at-home gatherings & then, when we were asked to teach a series of classes on entertaining for our local school board, we evolved into a travelling cooking school of sorts. For each of us this posed a challenge. Trained as a floral designer, Joyce did not see herself in the role of teacher, whereas, Carla, trained as an English teacher, questioned her ability to chop & talk at the same time. Solution? For the first while Joyce chopped & Carla talked. Later each of us learned to chop & talk. Clearly a celebration was in order! We left our husbands & families behind & went to San Francisco, note-pads in hand, to attend the first of many cooking classes. Since then we have sat at the feet of such cooking gurus as Jacques Pépin & Perla Meyers, as well as local chefs & cooks. Joyce experienced further "hands-on" training from Paris's La Varenne Cooking School when it offered classes in the United States. We are still teaching & always learning.

As Cooking & Company, we have presented classes for local school boards, department stores, cookware shops & women's groups. Along the way our "audiences" have given us a lot of enjoyment & an opportunity not only to hone our cooking skills, but to appreciate some of their needs as hosts. As a result, we are offering this book with YOU in mind.

These hors-d'oeuvre recipes are super, but, best of all, they can be prepared well ahead of time & refrigerated or frozen to await your guests. Our collection challenges the old definition of hors-d'oeuvres—they need not be delicately decorated morsels of food on tiny, toasted squares! These hors-d'oeuvres are contemporary—fresh, exciting, easy to prepare & beautifully satisfying to the hungriest eye. There are representatives from all branches of the family (local & international)—from dips & spreads, savoury pastries, meat & fish delicacies to unforgettable chicken drumsticks.

Hors-d'oeuvres are too delicious to be confined merely to their traditional role as pre-dinner snacks or cocktail party fare. *Hors-d'oeuvres* will carry you through your entertaining calendar: a Christmas cocktail buffet, a spontaneous après-sport gathering, a springtime brunch, a snack by the TV, a casual backyard feast, a child's birthday party, or a summertime picnic à deux. (We know that many of these recipes will become everyday favourites.) Treat your guests & yourself—serve hors-d'oeuvres for *any* occasion where friends, fun & food come together.

We have included a few extras as well—a selection of tasty additions to your table (homemade nibblers, nut mixes, mustards & versatile fillings for vegetables or pastries, to name a few), some liquid magic, sweet tooth pleasers, menu teasers & more. . . .

Hors-d'oeuvres lets you be a guest at your own party!

Carla and Joyce
Cooking & Company

For the most fun

Just a few suggestions we hope will help make your party planning easier:

♥Decide what kind of get-together it will be.

♥Create a menu (this can be the hardest part of entertaining & the most fun).

Keep the menu simple!
How many hors-d'oeuvres?

Before Dinner—1 or 2 different kinds should be enough, but allow several per person.

Cocktail party—about 6 to 9 per person with a good variety.

The larger the group, the more variety is needed. For a group of 15 to 20—3 or 4 different kinds. A nice balance would be 1 fish hors-d'oeuvre, 1 cheese & a vegetable platter with a dipping sauce.

♥Make a guest list (don't forget your own name).

♥Have your recipes in front of you when you are making your shopping list to avoid last minute dashes to the store.

♥Before beginning the preparation of your recipes *always* read through the entire recipe (ingredients & method) to familiarize yourself with the game plan.

♥In your mind's eye match up foods to be served with serving dishes. This will allow time to borrow extra trays, etc. & save last minute panic in the kitchen.

♥Be sure you have enough napkins, cocktail picks, glasses, ice & ashtrays, etc.

♥Don't forget your food table decor—a single flower or a grand centrepiece, baskets of plants, a grouping of candles, bowls of fruit or a basket of beautiful vegetables. Use your imagination—set a mood. Do give it some thought.

♥Give yourself some thought too—like what to wear. Choose something comfortable.

♥Hire some help if you can.

♥Planning well in advance will assure you success. Now sit back, relax & be a guest at your own party.

Dips & Spreads

Black Olive Spread

Yield: About 2 cups.

1 (14 oz./398 mL) tin pitted black olives, minced
½ cup mayonnaise
2 tbsp. minced onion
¼ tsp. curry powder
1 cup grated sharp Cheddar cheese
1 package English muffins

Mix the first 5 ingredients well. Spread on lightly toasted English muffin halves. Place under the broiler **3** to **4 minutes** until hot & bubbly. Quarter each muffin half.

This is also a good filling for savoury cream puffs (pâte à choux), Page 48 or Toast Rolls, Page 33

Camembert Cream

Yield: 2 rolls approx. 8 × 1½ inches.

10 oz. Camembert cheese, peeled & cut up
½ cup whipping cream (do not whip)
¼ cup butter
Salt to taste
⅛ to ¼ tsp. cayenne pepper
⅓ cup chopped walnuts or other nuts

Place all of the ingredients except the nuts in a food processor & blend well or mix by hand. Turn out & form into a ball or log. Roll in the nuts. Chill several hours or preferably overnight. Serve with water wafers or Melba toast.

This mixture can sometimes be a little soupy. If so, place in the refrigerator for about **20 minutes** to firm up before shaping.

Camembert Cream can also be frozen. Shape it into a log, freeze it, thaw slightly, slice it & serve—it has quite a different taste & presentation. Frozen it will keep about 2 weeks.

Life Expectancy: Two days maximum in the refrigerator.

Christmas Eve Chip Dip

Christmas Eve would not happen at the Palmers without this dip.

Yield: About 2 cups.

1 (8 oz./250 g) package plain cream cheese, softened
4 tbsp. ketchup
4 tbsp. mayonnaise
4 tbsp. finely chopped parsley
4 tbsp. finely chopped onion
2 tsp. Worcestershire sauce
1 tbsp. butter, softened
Pinch of salt

Combine the ingredients. Beat well. Chill. Make several hours ahead to allow the flavours to blend. If there is any left over, it will keep for several days in the refrigerator. Ripple chips make the best dippers.

Feta Cream

Yield: About 3 cups.

4 oz. Feta cheese
1½ cups butter
1 (8 oz./250 g) package plain cream cheese

Place the Feta cheese in a sieve & rinse well in cold water. Mix all of the ingredients together by hand or in a food processor until well combined. Pack into a crock or jar & chill. Serve with thin slices of coarse rye bread.

Life Expectancy: About 1 month in the refrigerator.

Orange Cream Cheese

Yield: About 1 cup.

1 (8 oz./250 g) package plain cream cheese, softened
1 tbsp. orange-flavoured liqueur (Grand Marnier, Triple
    Sec, Cointreau) or 1 tbsp. fresh orange juice
grated rind (zest▾) of 1 orange, finely chopped

Mix all of the ingredients together. Serve at room temperature with crackers or a plain cookie. Stuff into halves of dates or make sandwich cookies with digestive biscuits.

▾The ''zest'' of any citrus fruit is the coloured part of the rind. The white or pith layer tends to be bitter, so leave it behind. There is a gadget known as a ''zester'' which performs this function admirably provided you buy a good quality one. They make great Xmas stocking stuffers. Alternatively, employ a vegetable peeler or a paring knife.

Swiss Cheese Stacks

Yield: About 5 dozen.

1 cup butter, softened
⅓ cup Roquefort cheese
¼ cup chopped parsley
¼ cup chopped watercress
1 tsp. brandy
2 (8 oz./250 g) packages Swiss cheese slices

Cream together the butter & Roquefort cheese. Add the parsley, watercress & brandy. Mix until very smooth. Spread on the cheese slices. Place 1 piece of spread cheese on top of another to form a stack 5 or 6 slices high. Press together, wrap in plastic & chill well. To serve, cut into ½ inch squares & put on cocktail picks.

These can be made 3 or 4 days in advance.

Indonesian Cream

Yield: About 1 cup.

Spread on an unsalted cracker, this fast becomes an addiction. Serve with Tringles, Page 52.

1 (8 oz./250 g) package plain cream cheese, softened
½ cup shredded coconut
2 tbsp. hot chutney, chopped
½ tsp. curry powder
½ tsp. powdered ginger

By hand or in a food processor, cream the cheese & add the chutney, coconut, curry & ginger. Mix until well blended.

This will keep several days in the refrigerator.

Shrimp & Red Onion Spread

Served in a lettuce cup, this makes a tasty appetizer salad or luncheon treat.

Yield: About 2½ cups.

1 lb. small, cooked shrimp
½ cup mayonnaise (home-made preferred)
1½ tbsp. lemon juice
1 to 2 tbsp. sugar
½ cup sour cream or plain yogurt
½ cup chopped red onion
½ to 1 tsp. dried dill or 1 tbsp. fresh dill, chopped
a few grinds of pepper

Combine all the ingredients & refrigerate. Prepare at least a day in advance to allow flavours to blend. Taste & adjust the seasonings before serving.

To serve: Place in a bowl garnished with red onion rings & a sprig of fresh dill if available. Spoon onto Melba toast.

Antipasto

Make this with a friend: share the work & split the harvest.

Yield: About 12 pints.

2 packages frozen artichoke hearts, slightly cooked
1 small head cauliflower, slightly cooked & broken into
    small pieces
1 (35 oz./1 L) jar dill pickles
1 (14 oz./398 mL) tin green beans
1 (14 oz./398 mL) tin yellow beans
1 tin ripe olives, pitted
1 (375 mL) jar stuffed green olives or bits & pieces
2 tins mushrooms
4 tins tuna
2 green peppers, seeded
2 red peppers, seeded or 2 (250 mL) jars pimiento
3 tins anchovy fillets
¾ cup olive oil
½ cup vinegar
3¼ cups ketchup
½ cup sugar

Drain all canned goods & chop. The food processor can be helpful here if restraint is used—each vegetable should retain some identity. Mix all ingredients well. Pack into sterilized sealers. Process in boiling water bath for **30 minutes**. Start timing when the water returns to a boil. Serve with deep fried pasta shells, Page 59. Provide a spoon for filling the shells.

Guacamole Sauce

Yield: About 2 cups.

2 tbsp. chopped onion
1 large tomato, skinned & halved♥
3 tbsp. lemon juice
2 tbsp. olive oil
1 tbsp. mayonnaise
½ tsp. coriander leaves, crushed
Salt & freshly ground black pepper, to taste
1 ripe avocado, peeled, pitted & diced
1 tbsp. chopped canned jalapenos chili peppers
1½ tbsp. chopped parsley

Place the onion, half the tomato, 1 tbsp. of the lemon juice, the oil, mayonnaise, coriander, salt & pepper in a blender or food processor. Blend until smooth. Dice the remaining tomato half & combine in a bowl with the avocado, chili peppers, parsley & remaining lemon juice. Add the puréed mixture. Toss to mix well. Chill. Serve with taco or tortilla chips. Better still, try this with our recipe for Chili Doughnuts on Page 47.

♥ To peel a tomato, plunge it into boiling water for about **1 minute**. Remove & place under cold water for easy handling. The skin should slip off readily.

The Missing Recipe

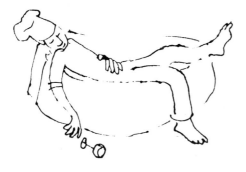

Hot Anchovy-Flavoured Dip
for Vegetables

In Italy this concoction is known as *bagna caôda*, literally, hot bath. Anyone whom we've known to be a confessed anchovy hater has become an anchovy lover after the first taste of this wonderful dip.

Yield: We serve this fondue-style as the first course of an Italian dinner for 6 or 8 people. Naturally, as one of several hors-d'oeuvres, it would serve more.

¾ cup olive oil
3 tbsp. butter
2 to 3 whole garlic cloves, peeled, halved & slightly
    crushed
1 (50 g) tin anchovy fillets, drained on paper towel,
    & chopped
¾ to 1 tsp. salt
1 loaf French bread, thickly sliced just before serving

A generous & colourful basket of raw vegetables, cleaned
& cut in dipping size pieces. Choose from artichokes,
asparagus, broccoli, cauliflower, carrots, celery, green
pepper, zucchini, snowpeas, mushrooms & radishes.
(Cocktail picks make good handles if needed.)

Just before serving, heat the oil, butter & garlic cloves in a fondue pot (ceramic preferred) over low heat until the butter is thoroughly melted. Remove the garlic when it is golden since beyond this point it burns easily. Add the anchovies. Continue to cook the mixture over low heat, stirring frequently until the anchovies dissolve. Add salt, stir & bring to the table along with the bread & vegetables. Set the fondue pot over a low flame to keep it hot, but never boiling.

Now the ritual of eating *bagna caôda:*
One hand takes a vegetable, the other a slice of bread. Dip the vegetable in the ''bath'', using the bread to catch the drips. Interrupt this rhythm only to enjoy some wine— Joyce prefers red, Carla white—as long as there's lots of it! After several sips & dunks enjoy the garlic bread (& more wine).

Herb Cheese *(Mock Boursin)*

Yield: About 2 cups.

2 (8 oz./250 g) packages plain cream cheese
2 tsp. milk
3 tbsp. parsley, finely chopped
1 tsp. onion powder
1 tsp. tarragon
A pinch each of oregano, garlic powder & seasoned salt

Beat well & store in the refrigerator overnight. Taste &
adjust the seasonings. Pack in a crock or make into a ball &
roll in chopped nuts, parsley, paprika or whatever. Wrap
well. This will keep about 1 week in the refrigerator.

This is easily doubled. Do not, however, double the
quantity of herbs. Increase to taste.

A ''pinch'' in the kitchen for a woman is said to be whatever she can pick
up between her thumb, middle & index fingers. For a man it is
whatever he can pick up between his thumb & index finger.

Hot Cheese Dip
or, as we like to call it,
Mexican Madness

This keeps for weeks in the refrigerator. The recipe can easily be halved.

Yield: Serves ''The Army'' (about 40).

3 lb. Velveeta type cheese
1 lb. sharp Cheddar cheese
8 cloves garlic, minced (yes, that's 8!)
2 onions, finely chopped
1 (3.5 oz./100 mL) tin jalapenos chili peppers, finely
    chopped
1 (28 oz./796 mL) tin tomatoes, finely chopped, plus
    the juice

Grate or cube the cheeses & place them in a large heavy casserole or ovenproof saucepan. Add the minced garlic & all of the very finely chopped vegetables plus the juice from the tomatoes. Mix together till well blended. Bake for **2** to **2½ hours** at **225°F**, stirring 3 or 4 times. Serve hot in a chafing dish or ceramic fondue pot. This is terrific with corn chips or tortilla chips. If you have a food processor, purée all the vegetables & garlic (excluding the juice from the tomatoes) & then add the mixture to the cheeses, along with the juice. Mix well. This is also good with a crudité. ♥

♥The word ''crudité'' refers to a selection of raw vegetables.

Hot Crab Dip

Yield: About 2½ cups.

1 cup mayonnaise
¼ cup finely chopped green onion
1 to 2 tsp. horseradish (depends on how hot you want it)
1 tbsp. lemon juice
1 tin crabmeat, rinsed & drained
⅓ cup toasted slivered almonds, pecans, or walnuts

Mix together all the ingredients except the nuts. Pour into a buttered ovenproof serving dish. Top with nuts. Bake at **300°F** about **20 minutes** or until hot & bubbly. Serve with assorted crisp crackers. Keep warm on a candle warmer. This should be made 1 day ahead for the flavours to blend. It can also be served cold as a spread.

Life Expectancy: 3 days in refrigerator if your family doesn't find it first.

Spicy Hot Shrimp Dip

Bring on the cold beer. This is delicious hot or cold.

Yield: About 2½ to 3 cups.

2 (8 oz./250 g) packages plain cream cheese, cut into
   chunks
1 tin shrimp, drained & rinsed
½ cup chopped green onions with some of the tops
1 medium tomato, peeled, seeded & chopped
1 or 2 garlic cloves, minced
2 hot banana peppers, finely chopped
1 or 2 chopped Torrido peppers (these are very hot)♥

Gently melt the cream cheese over hot water or in a heavy
saucepan over medium heat. Add the shrimp, green
onions, tomato, garlic & peppers. Pour into a chafing dish
& serve with tortilla chips.

Make this dip a day or two ahead, or at least several hours
before serving to allow the flavours to blend. It will keep
one week. It will last one night.

♥Torrido is the brand name for these hot chili peppers. They come in a
jar & can be found in the Mexican section of your food store.

Roquefort Cheese Dip

Yield: About 4 cups.

¼ lb. Roquefort cheese or blue cheese
2 cups sour cream
2 cups mayonnaise
1 clove garlic, finely chopped
2 tbsp. fresh lemon juice
½ cup buttermilk♥

Crumble the cheese & mix it together with the rest of the ingredients. Prepare several hours ahead, to allow the flavours to blend.

This makes a wonderful dressing for salads as well.

This will keep up to 3 weeks in the refrigerator.

♥ We use Pacific Cultured Buttermilk Powder (1½ tbsp. buttermilk powder added to the other ingredients plus ½ cup cold water).

We'll Name It Later Spread

Yield: About 2 cups.

½ cup chopped pecans, walnuts, almonds or mixture
thereof
¼ tsp. salt
2 tbsp. butter
1 (8 oz./250 g) package plain cream cheese, softened
2 tsp. milk
1 tbsp. grated onion
½ tsp. minced garlic
¼ tsp. black pepper (freshly ground preferred—about
3 twists)
½ cup sour cream
¼ lb. corned beef, chopped (packaged or our own,
Page 66)
¼ cup finely chopped green pepper

In a small fry-pan over medium heat, sauté the pecans in
butter & salt until golden brown. Set aside.

In a small mixing bowl, combine the cream cheese, milk,
onion, garlic, pepper & sour cream. Mix until smooth. Stir
in the beef, green pepper & nuts. Refrigerate until needed.
Serve on Melba toast, in celery stalks or what you will.

Curry Vegetable Dipping Sauce

Yield: About 4½ cups.

3 cups mayonnaise
1½ tsp. lemon juice
¾ cup finely chopped parsley
3 tbsp. finely chopped green onion, white part only
3 tbsp. fresh chives or green part from onion, finely
    chopped
1½ cups sour cream
¾ tsp. salt
1½ tsp. curry powder (more or less, depending on your
    taste)
½ tsp. garlic powder or 1 garlic clove, minced
1½ tsp. Worcestershire sauce

If preparing by hand, combine all of the ingredients & mix
well. In a food processor mince the parsley & green onion
(plus the garlic clove if used). Then add the remaining
ingredients & mix well. Store in a covered jar in the
refrigerator. Make this sauce **at least 24 hours** ahead of
time so the flavours will blend. The recipe can be halved
easily, but since this dip keeps for 3 weeks in the refrigerator,
why not make the full recipe? Raw vegetables & dipping
sauce spruce up any lunch time & kids love this dip!

To help give mushrooms a longer life, store them in a brown paper bag
in the refrigerator.

Fillings for Pastries, Vegetables & Sandwiches

Avocado & Salmon Filling

Try using this to stuff pâte à choux, cherry tomatoes or celery.

Yield: About 1 cup.

1 (7¾ oz./220 g) tin sockeye salmon, drained, bones & skin removed
1 avocado, peeled, pitted & mashed
¼ cup minced onion
1 tbsp. fresh lemon juice
Pepper to taste

Mix all of the ingredients together. Sneak a taste to check if salt is needed. Cover & refrigerate. Use within a couple of hours.

Mushroom filling for Turnovers, Page 39, or Tart, Page 41, can also be used to fill choux pastry.

Corned Beef & Green Pepper Filling

Yield: About 2 cups.

Use to fill pâte à choux, Page 48.

½ lb. corned beef, finely chopped
1 large green pepper, finely chopped
1 tsp. Tangy Mustard (Page 83), or Dijon mustard, to taste
¼ cup mayonnaise
Salt & pepper, to taste

Mix all of the ingredients together. Cover & refrigerate.
This will keep several days.

Other filling suggestions:
˅Grated sharp Cheddar, chopped olive, mayonnaise, salt
& pepper.

˅Cubes of Gruyère, Brie, or Camembert inserted in puffs
before reheating.

Curried Almond Chicken Filling

Yield: About 2½ cups.

1 cup finely chopped, cooked chicken♥
1 cup mayonnaise
⅓ cup almonds, lightly toasted & ground
¼ cup minced parsley
2 large shallots, minced♥♥
2 tsp. fresh lemon juice
1½ tsp. curry powder or to taste
Dash of Tabasco Sauce
Salt & pepper to taste

Combine all of the ingredients in a large bowl & blend well.
Cover & refrigerate. This will keep 2 to 3 days.

Yet another filling for pâte à choux, Page 48.

♥Try crabmeat or shrimp for fun.
♥♥Substitute for shallots, see Page 41.

Mustard Stuffed Eggs

Always popular, these add pizzazz to any table.

Yield: 8.

**4 hard-boiled eggs cut in half (yolks removed, whites
  reserved)**
1 tbsp. soft butter
1 tbsp. mayonnaise
2 tsp. mustard (try one of ours or use Dijon)
1 tsp. lemon juice
Salt & pepper to taste

Mix together all of the ingredients except the egg whites till
well blended. Cover & chill **30 minutes**. Put the mixture
into a pastry bag fitted with a fluted tip, & pipe the mixture
into the egg whites.

The filling is also good in cherry tomatoes (the egg whites
can be chopped & added to the mixture).

Smoked Salmon Stuffed Eggs

An economical way to add smoked salmon to your menu.

Yield: 8.

**4 hard-boiled eggs cut in ½ (yolks removed, whites
  reserved)**
3 oz. minced smoked salmon (⅓ cup)
¼ cup sour cream
1½ tbsp. lemon juice or to taste
Salt & pepper

Mix together all of the ingredients except the egg whites
in a food processor or blend together by hand. Chill,
covered, for **30 minutes**. Put the mixture into a pastry bag
& pipe it into the whites or use the old stand-by—a spoon.

Tuna & Caper Filling

Yield: About 1 cup.

**1 (7¾ oz./220 g) tin white flaked tuna, drained
2 to 3 tbsp. mayonnaise or enough to bind the mixture
2 tsp. French-Style Mustard (Page 82) or 1 tsp.Dijon
1½ tbsp. capers, drained**

In a bowl, mash the tuna, mayonnaise, mustard, capers, & mix thoroughly. Taste for seasoning. Add salt & pepper if needed. Cover & chill.

Make tiny corn muffins or baking powder biscuits. Split open, butter & fill with thin slices of smoked turkey & a dollop of cranberry sauce.

How about some real extravagance? Caviar—provide the knives for spreading, toast strips & lemon segments. Set the bowl of caviar in a larger bowl filled with ice. Très bon.

Toast Rolls

In the "olden days" rolled sandwiches were a must for afternoon tea. We've taken them out of that era & into the 1980s with zestier fillings & the added appeal of do-ahead-&- freeze. Use these anytime—as a late evening snack, an impromptu lunch, a soup accompaniment. . . .

Method of Attack:
Remove the crusts from slices of fresh bread. Roll with a rolling pin to flatten & thin the bread. (This helps make neater rolls.) Butter the bread lightly & spread the desired filling to the edges. Roll up jelly-roll fashion or make small sandwich fingers or squares. Wrap well in plastic wrap & freeze no longer than 2 weeks. Fillings, however, may be frozen for up to 2 months.

To bake: Preheat the oven to **375°F**. Cut frozen rolls in halves, thirds, or leave whole for heartier appetites & occasions. Place on baking sheets & brush with melted butter. Bake for about **5 minutes**, then broil until nicely toasted & bubbly. Watch carefully to avoid burning.

The Fillings

Clam Filling

Yield: About 8 rolls.

½ cup butter, softened
2 green onions, minced
2 tbsp. minced parsley
1 clove garlic, minced
½ tsp. lemon juice
1 tsp. dry white wine or vermouth
¼ tsp. salt
white pepper to taste
1 (10 oz./284 mL) tin baby clams, drained well

Mix all of the ingredients together & use to fill toast rolls. This recipe doubles easily.

Try as a filling for pâte à choux or mushroom caps & serve warm.

Cheddar-Cashew Filling

Yield: About 12 rolls.

This concoction also makes a great filling for celery & works well as a cheese ball.

1 (8 oz./250 g) package plain cream cheese, softened
4 oz./125 g sharp Cheddar cheese, shredded
½ cup chopped unsalted cashews, lightly toasted
2 tbsp. finely chopped parsley
dash of cayenne pepper

Combine the cream cheese, shredded Cheddar & cayenne. Beat until smooth. Stir in the toasted nuts & parsley. Use this as a filling for toast rolls.

Try making this with Stilton instead of Cheddar or toasted walnuts instead of cashews.

Niçoise-Style Filling

Yield: About 12 rolls.

1 (8 oz./250 g) package plain cream cheese, softened
¼ cup pitted & chopped Greek or black olives
¼ cup finely chopped pimiento
1½ tsp. anchovy paste
2 tsp. olive oil

Combine all of the ingredients. Blend well. Use this as a filling for toast rolls or try it as a filling for vegetables.

Bacon & Gruyère Filling

Yield: About 12 rolls.

½ lb. lean bacon
2 oz. Gruyère cheese, grated
½ cup mayonnaise
1 (10 oz./284 mL) tin mushrooms, drained & chopped
salt & pepper to taste

Cook the bacon until crisp. Drain it well on paper towels. Chop. In a bowl combine the remaining ingredients. Stir in the bacon. Use this as a filling for toast rolls.

These are especially good at brunch.

Spinach Filling

Yield: About 14 rolls.

⅓ cup finely chopped onion
1 clove garlic, minced
2 tbsp. butter
1 (10 oz./284 mL) package frozen spinach, cooked,
    squeezed dry & chopped
freshly grated nutmeg, salt & pepper to taste
4 oz./125 g plain cream cheese, softened & cut into
    chunks
1 tsp. Tangy Sweet Mustard, Page 83, or Dijon mustard

Optional: ¼" thick strips Gruyère or Cheddar cheese cut to
fit toast roll.

In a fry-pan, sauté the onion & garlic in butter over
medium heat, until softened. Add the spinach, freshly
grated nutmeg, salt & pepper & sauté about **2 minutes**,
stirring constantly. Add the cream cheese, stirring until
melted & well combined. Remove from heat, add the
mustard & stir. Cool slightly, spread on prepared bread,
place a cheese strip along 1 edge & roll up.

Mozzarella & Anchovy Filling

Yield: About 10 rolls.

4 oz./125 g Mozzarella cheese, grated
1 small (50 g) tin flat anchovy fillets, drained & minced
¼ cup butter, softened
1 tbsp. lemon juice
1 tbsp. minced parsley
1 small clove garlic, minced
freshly ground black pepper to taste

Mix all of the ingredients together & use as a filling for toast
rolls.

Experiment with other recipes for fillings in this book
—especially good à la toast roll are the Black Olive Spread
(Page 10) & the filling for Mushroom Turnovers (Page 39).

Pastry

Basic Pastry for Savouries *(Pâte Brisée)*

Yield: 2 8 or 9 inch pie shells or 2 dozen small tarts.

3 cups flour
2 tbsp. shortening
1 tsp. salt
¾ cup butter♥
6 to 7 tbsp. ice cold water

With a pastry blender, blend the shortening & butter with flour & salt until it resembles a very coarse meal. Add the water all at once & mix with a fork until it all comes into a ball. Wrap in plastic wrap & put in the refrigerator for at least **1 hour**. This can be frozen up to 2 months.

For sweet pastry add 1 tbsp. sugar.
Use for Mushroom Tart, Page 41, or Spinach Tart, Page 42.

♥Unsalted butter is preferred for pastry because its moisture content is less & its flavour is richer.

When making sausage rolls, paint the uncooked pastry with mustard or crabapple jelly. Add the meat, roll & bake.

Cream Cheese Pastry

This pastry is great to work with, can be made days ahead, & is a perfect base for sweets or savouries.

Yield: 5 to 6 dozen 2 inch tart shells.

1 cup soft butter
1 (8 oz./250 g) package plain cream cheese, softened
2 cups all-purpose flour

With a fork, cream the butter with the cream cheese. Mix in the flour. Form into a ball, wrap in plastic wrap or wax paper & chill 6 hours or longer. This freezes beautifully. Let the pastry soften a little before rolling.

Use for Mushroom Turnovers, Page 39, or Ginger Roll, Page 38.

For small tarts: Line the tart tins with pastry. Prick with a fork. Chill **1 hour** in the refrigerator or **15 minutes** in the freezer. Line the pastry with foil & fill with dried beans. Bake in a preheated **375°F** oven for **10 minutes**. Remove the foil & beans. Bake about another **10 minutes** or until lightly browned. Remove from the tins & cool. These can be frozen for later use. Fill as desired. This procedure is known as "blind baking." Use this method any time a baked pastry shell is called for & solve the mystery of the shrinking shell.

Variation: toasted & finely ground almonds, pecans, walnuts or hazelnuts added to pastry are an interesting touch.

Ginger Roll

This can be made ahead of time & frozen.
Take it out of the freezer & bake as you need it.

Yield: About 5 dozen slices.

1 recipe Cream Cheese Pastry, Page 37, chilled
1 lb. lean ground pork
½ cup flaked crab meat or 1 tin crab meat♥
½ tsp. salt
1 (8 oz./227 mL) tin water chestnuts, minced
2 green onions, minced, tops & all
2 tsp. grated fresh ginger root or ½ tsp. dry ground ginger
1½ tbsp. soy sauce
1 egg, beaten
¼ cup fine dry bread crumbs

Cook the ground pork in a fry-pan only until it looks white.
Drain the fat. Add the remaining ingredients & cook
5 minutes. Cool. Divide the pastry into 4 parts. On a lightly
floured surface roll out each piece into a rectangle about
12 × 9 inches. Cut these in half lengthwise, & spread each
piece with filling. From the long side, roll up tightly like
a jelly roll. Moisten the edges with water; press to seal.
Place the rolls on a cookie sheet; chill 1 hour. Cut into
1 inch slices. Bake in a preheated **375°F** oven for **20** to
25 minutes. Serve warm or cold.

To freeze, roll, wrap & freeze. To bake, let stand at room
temperature for about **15 minutes**. Slice & place on a
cookie sheet. Bake as above.

♥Cooked ground chicken or ground beef can be substituted.

Mushroom Turnovers

Yield: Approximately 85.

1 recipe Cream Cheese Pastry, Page 37, chilled
½ lb. fresh mushrooms, minced
3 tbsp. butter
1 large onion, minced
1 tsp. salt
¼ tsp. thyme
2 tbsp. flour
¼ cup sour cream

1 egg beaten with 1 tbsp. water for glaze

In a fry-pan, sauté the minced mushrooms in butter, add the onion & cook until tender. Stir in the salt, thyme & flour. Cook **1** to **2 minutes**. Remove from heat & stir in the sour cream. Cool.

Roll out the dough on a lightly floured surface. Cut the dough into 2 inch circles. Place ½ tsp. of the cooled mushroom mixture on each circle & fold the circle in half. Press the edges together with the tines of a fork; prick the top with the fork. If you wish to freeze them, now is the time. To bake, place on an ungreased cookie sheet, & brush the tops with beaten egg. Bake at **450°F** for **12 minutes** or until light brown. Serve hot. If they have been frozen, thaw for **20 minutes** & bake as above.

Depending on the amount of moisture given off from the mushrooms you may find you have to add a little extra milk or light cream to the mixture to make it creamy (not soupy!).

One ¼ oz. (7 g) package of dried mushrooms (Cèpes) added to this gives a richer mushroom flavour. To use dried mushrooms: rinse in cold water then soak in 1 cup warm water for ½ **hour** to soften. Drain & reserve the liquid. (You may find some grit at the bottom of the liquid.) Chop the mushrooms. Add to the mixture before the seasonings & flour. Add some of the reserved liquid if needed. This liquid can be frozen. Added to a beef stew, it's super.

Sardine Fingers

Yield: About 4 dozen.

1 recipe Cream Cheese Pastry, Page 37, chilled
2 tins sardines, drained of most of their oil
4 tbsp. lemon juice
2 tbsp. finely chopped onion
1½ tbsp. anchovy paste
1 tsp. dill weed

1 egg beaten with 1 tbsp. water for glaze

Mash the sardines together with the lemon juice, onion, anchovy paste & dill weed.

Cut the pastry into 4 pieces. Roll out each piece into a rectangle about 8 × 12 inches & about ⅛ inch thick. Cut in half lengthwise. (You now have 2 pieces 4 × 12 inches.) Brush some egg glaze onto rectangle, let sit for a few seconds, then spread some sardine mixture on the pastry, spreading to the edges. Top with the second 4 × 12 inch rectangle. ♥ Cut into 1 inch wide fingers, brush with some egg glaze & place on an ungreased baking sheet. Repeat with the remaining pastry & filling.

Bake in a preheated **400°F** oven **10** to **15 minutes** or until the pastry is nicely browned. Serve hot or at room temperature. These can be frozen before or after baking.

♥ If the pastry softens, place it in the refrigerator for **10** to **15 minutes** to firm up before slicing into finger shapes.

Mushroom Tart

This pie can be baked a day ahead & reheated or prepared a day ahead & baked just before serving.

Yield: One 9 or 10 inch tart.

1 recipe Pâte Brisée, Page 36

2 tbsp. butter
1 onion, finely chopped
½ lb. mushrooms, finely chopped
2 shallots, finely chopped ♥
2 tbsp. flour
1½ cups light cream
Pinch grated nutmeg
Salt & pepper
3 egg yolks
2 tbsp. chopped parsley

1 egg beaten together with ½ tsp. salt to make glaze.

Melt the butter in a heavy based fry-pan. Add the onion & cook over medium heat until soft but not brown. Stir in the mushrooms & cook rapidly, stirring occasionally until all the moisture has evaporated. Stir in the shallots & continue cooking **1 minute**. Stir in the flour, add the cream, nutmeg, salt & pepper. Cook, stirring until the mixture thickens & simmer **2 minutes**. Remove from the heat & beat in the egg yolks. Add parsley & taste for seasoning. **Cool** completely.

Set the oven at **400°F**. Roll out ⅔ of the pastry dough & line an ungreased 9 or 10 inch pie pan or flan ring. Prick the bottom lightly with a fork & chill. Spread the cooled filling into the shell. Roll out the remaining dough & cut into thin strips. Make a lattice topping, pressing well into the edges of the pie shell to seal them. Brush with the egg glaze. Bake **30** to **40 minutes** or until nicely browned. Serve in thin wedges for a cocktail buffet or larger portions for lunch or brunch or what have you.

♥ Two or three green onions (white only) & ½ tsp. minced garlic are a good substitute for 2 shallots.

Spinach Tart

Don't shy away from this taste sensation because of the goat cheese. It's delicious. We kid you not.

1 10 inch tart shell of Pâte Brisée, Page 36, baked & cooled♥

3 tbsp. minced green onion
2 tbsp. butter
1½ cups cooked, well drained, chopped fresh spinach
**   or 2 (10 oz./284 mL) packages frozen spinach, cooked,**
**   drained & chopped**
¼ tsp. nutmeg
¼ tsp. each salt & pepper
4 oz./125 g plain cream cheese
¼ lb./125 g goat cheese♥♥
4 eggs, separated
½ cup whipping cream or half & half
⅓ cup fresh bread crumbs

Melt the butter in a fry-pan over low heat. Add the green onion, spinach, nutmeg, salt & pepper. Cook **5 minutes**. Remove from heat.

Cream the cheeses in a large bowl or food processor. Add the egg yolks one at a time, mixing well. Add the cream & spinach mixture & combine well. Beat 4 egg whites with a pinch of salt until they hold stiff peaks. Fold carefully into the spinach mixture. Pour the mixture into a baked tart shell. Dot top with 1 tbsp. butter & sprinkle with bread crumbs. Bake in a **375°F** oven for about **25 minutes**, or until top is puffed & browned. This can be frozen. To reheat, place in cold oven. Set oven to **375°F** & bake about **20 minutes**, or till thawed & heated through.

♥For instructions on how to ''blind bake'' a pie shell, see the recipe for Cream Cheese Pastry, Page 37.

♥♥We use a French goat cheese (Chèvre, for example). Try Feta cheese, but expect a stronger flavour.

Cheese Tarts

Yield: About 3 dozen.

1 recipe Pâte Brisée, Page 36

Make small tarts (the 2 inch size is nice for this recipe) according to the instructions on Page 37.

Filling:
⅔ cup milk
½ tsp. salt
2 egg yolks
1 tbsp. Tangy Sweet Mustard (Page 83)
1 tsp. cornstarch
a few good grinds of pepper
3 oz. grated Swiss cheese
½ cup whipping cream, whipped stiff
½ cup ground blanched almonds

Heat milk till bubbles form around the edge of the saucepan. Remove from heat.

In a bowl, mix together the egg yolks, salt, mustard, cornstarch & pepper. Add some of the hot milk to this mixture, stirring well. Pour this egg mixture slowly back into the hot milk. Cook over moderately low heat until thick & smooth. Remove from heat & add the grated cheese. Stir gently until the cheese melts. Cover with buttered wax paper & cool. Fold the whipped cream into the cooled cheese mixture. Transfer to a pastry bag fitted with a decorative tip & pipe into the baked & cooled pastry shells (or spoon the mixture into the shells). Sprinkle the tops with ground blanched almonds. Place in the refrigerator to chill.

To freeze:
Place the finished tarts on a baking sheet. Freeze. Pack into storage containers. These will keep about 1 month. Serve at room temperature.

Mediterranean Pastries

Yield: About 4 dozen.

1 recipe Pâte Brisée, Page 36, or your favourite pastry

2 tbsp. olive oil
1 cup finely chopped onion
½ cup finely chopped red pepper or pimiento
½ cup finely chopped green pepper
½ cup finely chopped zucchini, unpeeled
1 clove garlic, finely chopped
1 tsp. basil
½ tsp. oregano
½ tsp. salt
Cayenne pepper to taste
1 tbsp. flour
½ lb. tomatoes, peeled, seeded & chopped
¼ cup finely chopped parsley
1 tbsp. lemon juice
½ cup freshly grated Parmesan cheese

1 egg beaten with 1 tbsp. water for glaze.

In a fry-pan, heat the oil; then add the onion, peppers, zucchini, garlic, basil, oregano, salt & cayenne. Cover & cook about **20 minutes** until the vegetables are tender. Add the flour & cook, stirring constantly, for about **1 minute**. Add the tomatoes & cook about **10 minutes** or until the mixture is thick. Remove from heat; add the parsley, lemon juice & Parmesan, mixing well & carefully. Cool completely.

Roll out the pastry on a lightly floured surface. Cut with a 2 inch cookie cutter & place about 2 tsp. of filling on each round. Moisten the edges with a little water; then top with a second round, pressing lightly at the edges to seal. Place on baking sheets & if you like, now is the time to freeze these for social security. If not, brush each pastry with some glaze & bake in a preheated **400°F** oven for **15** to **20 minutes** or until golden. They may be frozen after baking & reheated in a **350°F** oven till heated through.

Stuffed Cucumber Cups

A nice fresh taste & colourful too.

Yield: About 4 dozen.

2 to 3 cucumbers (English preferred), unpeeled
1 recipe of Herb Cheese (Page 20)
¼ lb. smoked salmon, cut into thin strips about
**   1¼ × ¼ inches**
Fresh parsley

Score the cucumbers♥ with a fork & slice them into ½ inch
thick rounds. Using a spoon or paring knife, cut a shallow
cup in the top of each round.♥♥ Wrap the cucumbers in
paper towels & refrigerate for several hours to remove
excess moisture.

Fill each round with cheese, mounding it slightly. Crisscross
the top of each round with two strips of salmon. Garnish
with a small sprig of parsley. Refrigerate, covered, until
serving time.

♥ To ''score'' a cucumber: Run the tines of a fork lengthwise down the
cucumber. This will give the slices a decorative edge.

♥♥ A melon baller works really well.

Chutney Chicken Puffs

Yield: About 5 dozen.

1 cup chicken broth
½ cup butter
½ tsp. ground celery seed
½ tsp. cayenne pepper
1 tsp. Worcestershire sauce
1 tsp. salt
1 cup flour
4 eggs
1 loosely packed cup cooked chicken, chopped
½ cup toasted almonds, chopped
2 tbsp. chopped parsley
4 generous tbsp. hot chutney (such as Major Grey or
   Burgess Hot Bengal Chutney)

Place the broth, butter (cut into pieces), celery seed, cayenne, Worcestershire sauce & salt in a heavy saucepan. Bring to a boil. When the butter is completely melted, remove from heat & add the flour all at once. Mix rapidly with a wooden spoon until the dough forms a ball.

Place the pan back on low heat & cook **1** to **2 minutes**, stirring constantly. Transfer the mixture to a food processor or electric mixer bowl. Add the eggs, **one at a time**, mixing well after each addition so that the mixture is smooth before the next egg is added.

Stir in the chicken, almonds, parsley & chutney. Mix well. Drop by the teaspoonful about 1 inch apart onto greased baking sheets. Bake in a preheated **400°F** oven for **5 minutes**; then reduce the oven temperature to **375°F** & continue to bake for about **15 minutes** longer. Cool slightly, remove from baking sheets & store in a tightly covered container in the refrigerator or freeze for later use. When ready to use, place the frozen puffs on a baking sheet & warm in a **350°F** oven for about **10 minutes**. Serve warm or at room temperature.

Variation?
Use preserved ginger in syrup instead of the hot chutney. Remove the ginger from the syrup & chop finely before adding it to the dough.

Chili Doughnuts with Guacamole Sauce

Yield: About 3 dozen, depending on their size.

Chili:
2 tbsp. oil
1 onion, finely chopped
1 clove garlic, finely chopped
¾ lb. lean ground beef
2 tbsp. chili powder
1 tbsp. cumin
½ tsp. salt
⅛ tsp. cayenne pepper
3 tbsp. tomato paste

Doughnuts:
2 cups flour
½ tsp. salt
3 tsp. baking powder
¾ cup milk
2 eggs
¼ cup oil
Oil for deep frying—375°F
(Use deep-fry thermometer)♥

To prepare the chili: heat the oil in a heavy fry-pan & sauté the onions & garlic until tender. Do not brown. Add the ground beef & cook, stirring, until meat loses its red colour. Add the remaining ingredients & cook, stirring, until well blended, about **3 to 5 minutes**. Cool. Drain off the excess grease or liquid.

To prepare the doughnuts: Sift together the flour, salt & baking powder. Add the milk, eggs & ¼ cup oil & beat until smooth. Fold in the cooled, drained chili. Check the consistency of the mixture by making a trial doughnut. Drop a teaspoonful into the hot oil. If the dough is too stiff, stir in more milk & if the dough is too thin to retain its shape, whisk in a small quantity of flour. Deep fry (**375°**) by the teaspoonful, cooking about **1 to 2 minutes**. When the dough rises to the top, turn it over to finish cooking. Drain on paper towels.

Serve hot with guacamole sauce, Page 17.

To Freeze: Place on a baking sheet till firm. Pack into a container or bags. To reheat, bake the frozen doughnuts in a preheated **350°F** oven for **10 to 15 minutes** or until heated through.

♥If you don't have a thermometer, test the oil with a 1 inch cube of bread. This will brown in 1 minute if the oil is the right temperature.

Pâte à Choux

Commonly known as ''cream puff paste,'' pâte à choux is easily made from simple ingredients. Once formed & baked, these puffs wait patiently in the freezer until you are ready to fill them & they accommodate themselves to an endless variety of fillings from the sublime to whatever you have on hand. No freezer should be without them.

Yield: About 60.

1 cup water
½ cup butter, cut into pieces
Dash of salt
1 cup all-purpose flour
4 large eggs at room temperature

1 egg, beaten with 1 tbsp. water to make a glaze

Preheat the oven to **400°F**. Grease 2 baking sheets.

Place the water, butter & salt in a heavy saucepan. Bring to a boil. When the butter is completely melted, remove the pan from the heat & add the flour all at once. Mix rapidly with a wooden spoon until the dough forms a ball.

Place the pan back on low heat & cook **1** to **2 minutes**, stirring constantly. Transfer the mixture to a food processor or electric mixer bowl. Add the eggs, **one at a time**, beating well after each addition so that the mixture is smooth before the next egg is added.

Drop by the teaspoonful about 2 inches apart on greased baking sheets or fill a pastry bag fitted with a plain tube with the dough & pipe out 1 inch rounds or 2 inch éclairs (oblongs). Brush the puffs with the egg glaze to give them a shiny top. (Be careful not to spill any glaze on the baking sheets as this will make the puffs difficult to remove.)

Bake in a preheated oven at **400°F** for about **20 to 25 minutes** or until nicely browned. Remove from the oven, cut the tops & remove any unbaked batter. Put back in turned-off oven for about **5 minutes** to dry. Cool, fill & serve.

To Freeze: Place the cooled puffs on a baking sheet & freeze till firm. Remove & put in a storage container. When ready to use, place the frozen puffs on a baking sheet & warm in a **325°F** oven for about **10 minutes**.

For filling suggestions, see Pages 10, 27, 28 & 85.
To prevent puffs from becoming soggy, avoid filling them until about ½ hour before serving.

Pâte à Choux Variations
Herbed Gougères

Yield: About 60.

1 recipe Pâte à Choux, Page 48.

½ tsp. nutmeg (freshly grated, if possible)
1 tsp. salt
¼ tsp. white pepper
4 oz. Gruyère, grated (1 cup)
2 green onions, finely minced
1 tbsp. finely minced parsley
1 tsp. dried dillweed

1 egg, mixed with ½ tsp. salt

Preheat oven to **400°F**. Grease 2 baking sheets. Make 1 recipe of pâte à choux & add the remaining ingredients to the paste after the eggs have been added. Mix well. Form the puffs as in the basic recipe. Apply the egg glaze. Bake in a preheated **400°F** oven **20 to 25 minutes** or until nicely browned. Serve warm as is or cool slightly, slit sides & insert pimiento-stuffed olives. Without the olives these freeze beautifully.

Practise using a pastry bag by filling it with prepared instant mashed potatoes—an inexpensive & fun way to learn how to make all those fancy curlicues. Children love doing this too.

Gouda Shrimp Balls

Yield: About 60.

1 recipe Pâte à Choux, Page 48.

8 oz./250 g medium Gouda cheese, grated (2 cups)
2 tbsp. finely chopped green onion (green included)
or 2 tbsp. chopped fresh chives
2 (7¾ oz./220 g) tins of broken shrimp, well rinsed & any
    shell removed
4 dashes of Tabasco Sauce
1 tsp. salt
½ tsp. ground white pepper
Oil for deep frying—375°F

Make 1 recipe of pâte à choux & add the remaining
ingredients to the paste after the eggs have been added.
Drop by the teaspoonsful into hot oil & cook until golden.
Drain on paper towels. Serve warm. To freeze, place cooled
balls on baking sheets. Freeze until firm. Remove & place
in plastic bags to store. To bake: place frozen balls on
baking sheet in preheated **350°F** oven for about
10 minutes.

A wonderful air freshener for your home: In a saucepan of water place
about 2 tsp. of cinnamon or 2 or 3 broken cinnamon sticks, 1 tbsp.
whole cloves, 2 or 3 slices of lemon or orange. Simmer gently. Truly a
delightful fragrance!

Cocktail Biscuits

Yield: About 6 to 7 dozen.

Mushroom Mixture:
¼ cup butter
3 cups finely chopped mushrooms (about ¾ lb.)
6 shallots, minced♥
Salt & pepper
1½ cups finely chopped smoked ham
6 green onions, finely chopped

Biscuit:
4½ cups all-purpose flour
3 tbsp. baking powder
1½ tsp. salt
1½ cups butter, cut into small chunks
7 tbsp. solid shortening
1½ cups cold milk

Melt ¼ cup butter in a large fry-pan. Add the mushrooms
& shallots & sauté until the mushrooms are lightly
browned, about **8** to **10 minutes**. Season to taste with salt
& pepper. Set aside until cool.

Combine the flour, baking powder & salt in a large bowl.
With a pastry blender, cut in the butter & shortening until
the mixture resembles coarse meal. Add the milk. Using a
fork, combine just until the mixture begins to hold together
& form a ball. Add the mushroom mixture, ham & green
onions. Knead together.

Preheat the oven to **400°F**. Grease the baking sheets.
Generously flour your hands & shape the dough into 1 inch
balls; place on the baking sheets. Flatten slightly. Bake
15 minutes or until golden brown. Serve warm or at room
temperature. These can be frozen. To reheat, place the
frozen biscuits on an ungreased baking sheet in a preheated **350°F** oven for about **10 minutes** or until heated
through.

♥See Page 41 for a substitute.

The Victorian Mrs. Beeton said, ''Thrust an oniony knife into the earth to
take away the smell''.

Tringles or What-You-Wills

Sure to trigger guessing games. A must with Indonesian Cream, Page 14.

Cover 24 soda crackers with water & soak about **15 minutes**. Carefully remove them from the water & place on paper towels. Pat them dry & then cut them in half, diagonally. Transfer them to a lightly buttered baking sheet. (It's all in the way you hold your mouth. But, seriously, these guys are most forgiving & if one does break in transit, you can easily stick it back together & it will ''glue'' during the baking process.) Bake at **400°F** for about **20 minutes** or until nicely browned & crisped. Remove from the baking sheet & cool. Store in non-plastic containers.

Variations?
Sprinkle baked crackers with grated Parmesan.

Soak crackers in apple juice instead of water & when they are baked, sprinkle them with cinnamon. These make one of the best alternatives to apple pie that a dieter could hope for!

Gruyère Shortbread

Yield: About 3 dozen.

Make well ahead & store in the refrigerator or freezer.

1½ cups flour
½ tsp. salt
½ cup butter, softened
¼ lb. Gruyère cheese, grated
½ cup ground nuts (walnuts, almonds, pecans,
   macadamias or a combination)
1 egg

Blend the butter, cheese & egg. Gradually work in the flour & nuts. Mold into a roll 1½ inches in diameter. Wrap in wax paper & chill until firm. Slice ¼ inch thick. Place on lightly buttered baking sheets & bake in a preheated **400°F** oven for about **10 to 15 minutes** or until browned. To prepare ahead: bake & freeze. Reheat in a **400°F** oven for a **few minutes** before serving.

Whole Wheat Cheddar Hearts

Yield: About 3 dozen.

1 cup whole wheat flour
¼ cup wheat germ
½ tsp. salt
4 tbsp. butter
1 cup grated sharp Cheddar cheese
¼ cup ground, toasted walnuts (toast before grinding)
1 egg
dash of Tabasco Sauce
1½ to 2 tbsp. ice water

Combine the flour, wheat germ & salt in a bowl. Using a pastry blender, cut in the butter until the mixture resembles coarse meal. Stir in the cheese, walnuts, egg & Tabasco & enough water to form a soft dough. Chill about **30 minutes**. Preheat the oven to **375°F**. Roll out the dough to ¼ inch thickness on a lightly floured surface. Cut with a 2 inch heart-shaped cutter & place on lightly greased baking sheets. Bake **12** to **15 minutes** or until lightly browned.

These may be frozen after baking.

Onion Wafers

Yield: About 3 dozen.

These are easily prepared in a food processor.

1½ cups flour
½ tsp. salt
½ cup butter, chilled
4 oz./125 g plain cream cheese
4 green onions, minced
1 tsp. dried chervil
1 tsp. dried tarragon
1 egg, separated (white reserved)
coarse salt

Cream the butter & cheese together. Add the flour, salt, onion, herbs & egg yolk. Mix together to form a smooth dough. Shape into a cylinder, wrap well in plastic wrap & chill about **1 hour**, or freeze for later use.♥

Preheat the oven to **375°F**. Cut dough into ¼ inch slices. Place on lightly greased baking sheets & brush with slightly beaten egg white. Sprinkle with coarse salt. Bake **10** to **12 minutes** or until nicely browned. Serve at room temperature or freeze for a rainy day.

♥Remove from the freezer at least ½ hour before baking to allow for easy slicing.

Stilton Wafers

Yield: About 4 dozen.

1⅓ cups flour
⅓ cup butter, softened
4 oz./125 g Stilton cheese, crumbled
4 tbsp. sour cream

Cream the butter & Stilton together. Add the flour & sour cream & mix until a smooth dough forms.

Shape the dough into 2 logs about 1¼ inch in diameter. Wrap in plastic & chill for about 1 hour. Cut the logs into ¼ inch slices & bake in a preheated **350°F** oven **15** to **20 minutes** or until lightly browned. Cool & serve.

These can be frozen in log form if desired. Thaw enough to make slicing easy, cut into slices & bake as directed. Or freeze after baking.

Chèvre cheese may be used in place of Stilton.

A cheese wafer served with a drink whets the appetite nicely before a large dinner. Too many hors-d'oeuvres spoil the broth (so to speak).

Cheese Swirls

Yield: About 5 dozen.

2 (8 oz./250 g) packages plain cream cheese
2 tsp. milk or cream
½ tsp. garlic salt
¼ tsp. onion salt
¼ tsp. Worcestershire sauce
2 boxes Melba toast rounds or squares

Combine the ingredients. Mix well. Divide evenly into three bowls.

To the first bowl add:

1 tin broken shrimp, very finely chopped
½ tsp. fresh lemon juice
pinch of dried dill weed

Mix well.

To the next bowl add:
½ cup very finely chopped mushrooms
pinch of dried marjoram

Mix well.

To the final bowl add:
1 tin smoked oysters, well drained, very finely chopped
½ tsp. fresh lemon juice

Mix well.

Place each mixture in a piping bag with a star tip & pipe in swirls or mound with a spoon onto Melba toast. For ease in piping, make sure that the ingredients are very finely chopped. Freeze on a baking sheet. When frozen, pack them in storage containers if they are not to be used immediately. Bake frozen in a preheated **375°F** oven, about **10 minutes**.

Variation: Another coup for cherry tomatoes & celery.

Make your own garlic salt: ½ cup salt, 1 large, whole garlic clove, peeled. Place the salt & garlic clove in a glass jar. Cover & leave about 3 days. Remove the garlic.

Baked Cheese Puffs

Yield: About 36.

1 unsliced loaf day-old white or whole wheat bread,
    (crusts trimmed) cut into 1 inch cubes.
 ½ cup butter
4 oz./125 g plain cream cheese
¼ lb. sharp Cheddar cheese, grated
2 egg whites♥
¼ tsp. dry mustard
⅛ tsp. cayenne pepper
Salt & pepper to taste

Heat everything except the bread cubes & egg whites over
low heat until the cheese melts & the ingredients are well
combined. Beat the egg whites until stiff. Spoon some of
the cheese mixture into the beaten egg whites. Gently fold
the egg white mixture into the remaining cheese mixture.
Place over hot but not boiling water.

Dip the bread cubes into the mixture, coating well, letting
any excess drip back into the bowl. Place on a wax-paper-
lined baking sheet. Freeze. When frozen, place in a storage
container or in freezer bags. Bake frozen puffs in a
preheated oven, **400°F**, for **8 to 10 minutes** or until
golden.

♥ Now that you have two egg yolks left over you can make a batch of Ice
Cream Cookies on Page 89.

Marmalade & Bacon Canapé: Toast slices of bread, remove crusts &
cut in four. Let cool. Spread with a thin coat of mustard, top with slices
of crisply cooked, well drained bacon. Add a dollop of marmalade.

Sweet & Sour Bow Ties

From our San Francisco daze—a fun learning experience at cooking school.

Yield: About 2½ cups sauce.

The Bow Ties:
1 package won ton wrappers
Oil for deep frying—375°F

Dip a pastry brush in water & paint a ½ inch strip down the centre of each won ton wrapper. Gather into a bow tie & twist slightly. Deep fry for about **1 minute** per side or until golden. Drain on paper towels. Serve warm to scoop up the sweet & sour sauce. These freeze well. To reheat, bake frozen on a cookie sheet in preheated **375°F** oven for about **10 minutes** until thoroughly heated.

The Sauce:
2 cups crushed pineapple with juice
2 tbsp. tomato sauce
2 tbsp. soy sauce
½ cup apricot preserves
1 tbsp. cornstarch
¼ cup water
4 green onions, finely chopped
½ green pepper, finely chopped
¼ tsp. powdered ginger
Salt, pepper & chili powder to taste
Dash of ground cumin

Drain the pineapple, reserving the juice. Mix the juice, tomato sauce & preserves in a saucepan over medium-low heat, stirring constantly until well blended. Mix the cornstarch in the water & add to the saucepan. Cook until thickened. Add the green onion & green pepper & cook **10 minutes**. Season to taste. Add the pineapple. Serve warm or cool & freeze for later use.

Deep-Fried Pasta Shells
(Italian Potato Chips?)

Unusual & terrific! Make days ahead & hide.

1 lb./500 g package large pasta sea shells
Salt
Oil for deep frying—375°F

Cook the shells in boiling salted water **10** to **12 minutes**.
Don't overcook. Drain & dry on paper towels. Deep fry in
hot oil in small batches. Drain on paper towels. Salt while
still warm. Serve with Antipasto (Page 16) or as an
alternative to chips.

A 1 inch cube of white bread will turn golden brown in hot oil.

345° - 355°F - 65 sec
355° - 365°F - 60 sec
365° - 375°F - 55 sec
375° - 385°F - 40 sec
385° - 395°F - 20 sec

For your next pizza party: order plain cheese pizzas. Offer an array of
toppings so guests can "dress" their own.

Spinach Pâté

This is a terrifically versatile dish.

Yield: 1 8 × 4 inch or 9 × 5 inch loaf

3 (10 oz./284 mL) packages spinach, thawed
1 tbsp. butter
½ cup finely chopped onion
2 cups finely chopped mushrooms
1 large clove garlic, minced
3 tbsp. dry white wine or chicken broth
1 tsp. thyme
3 eggs
½ cup milk
⅛ tsp. nutmeg, freshly grated preferred
1 tsp. oregano
1 tbsp. lime or lemon juice
¼ cup finely chopped parsley
¼ cup freshly grated Parmesan cheese
½ cup bread crumbs
Salt & pepper to taste

Squeeze out as much of the moisture in the spinach as
possible. Chop very finely. Set aside in a large bowl. Butter
an 8 × 4 inch or 9 × 5 inch loaf pan. Heat the butter in a
large pan, but do not allow it to brown. Sauté the onion
until soft, but not brown. Add the mushrooms, garlic, wine
& thyme & cook over medium heat until the mushrooms
are cooked & the liquid has evaporated. Remove from heat
& add to the spinach.

Mix the eggs, milk & remaining ingredients together & add
to the spinach mixture, combining well. Pour into the
prepared pan, cover with buttered foil & bake at **350°F** for
about **45 minutes** or until firm. Remove from the oven, let
cool, then unmold. Serve cold in slices for a cocktail buffet.
This can be frozen.

Served hot, this makes a nice side dish for baked ham. At
your next brunch: slice, then heat gently (covered with
lettuce leaves to prevent moisture loss) in a **300°F** oven till
warm through. Place on top of toasted English muffins, top
with poached or scrambled eggs & your favourite sauce—
tomato, mushroom or hollandaise.

Mini Omelettes

Yield: 14 to 16 2 inch omelettes.

½ cup melted butter
4 eggs, lightly beaten
2 dashes Tabasco Sauce
Salt & pepper to taste
1 (10 oz./284 mL) package frozen spinach, thawed
⅓ cup diced pimiento
1 to 2 tbsp. chopped shallots or green onion
2 tbsp. Parmesan cheese

Preheat oven to **400°F**. Brush 2 inch muffin tins with melted butter. Thaw the spinach & squeeze out the excess moisture. Chop finely. Mix the eggs, seasonings, spinach, pimiento & shallots together. Place the buttered muffin tins in the preheated oven till the butter is hot. Remove from the oven & spoon about 2 tbsp. of the egg mixture into each cavity. Bake about **5 minutes** or until the mixture starts to pull away from the sides of the tin. Brush with additional melted butter & sprinkle with Parmesan cheese. Place under the broiler for a few seconds until the cheese melts. (Watch carefully, as these can burn easily.) Remove from tins & serve hot or at room temperature.

These can be made early in the morning of the day you crave them. Try making them in larger muffin tins & serve them for brunch with a good tomato or mushroom sauce . . . wonderful!

Terrine of Fresh Vegetables

Yield: One 9 × 5 inch loaf.

The crunchy freshness & lively colours in this mold make it a sure success on a cocktail buffet table. Served for lunch, it's a winner too!

1 cup finely diced green pepper
2 cups finely diced English cucumber, unpeeled
2 cups finely diced tomato˅
¾ cup finely diced red onion
1 cup finely diced celery
2 packages or 2 tbsp. unflavoured gelatin
4 tbsp. cold water
1 cup hot chicken stock˅˅
1 cup mayonnaise
1 tsp. salt
½ tsp. Tabasco Sauce
½ tsp dry mustard
1 tbsp. lemon juice

Wash & prepare the vegetables as indicated above. Set them aside in a large bowl. Dissolve the gelatin in cold water, then add the hot chicken stock slowly, stirring well to dissolve the gelatin totally. Let cool slightly, then combine with the mayonnaise in a large bowl. Mix well & add the salt, Tabasco, dry mustard & lemon juice. Add the vegetables & combine well.

Rinse a 9 × 5 × 3 inch loaf pan in cold water. Pour the vegetable mixture into the pan & chill until set—about **2 hours**.

Why not "gild the lily" & add ½ lb. fresh small shrimp, cooked, or 2 4oz. tins of shrimp, rinsed & drained?

˅ Peel & seed the tomato before chopping.

˅˅ If using tinned chicken stock, you may want to use ½ cup of the stock plus ½ cup of water.

Fish, Meat & Poultry

Seviche

Spanish in origin, here is an example of marinating leading to magic!

Yield: About 50 marinated morsels.

2 lb. halibut fillets, cut into ¾ inch cubes or
    2 lb. scallops, halved if large
¾ cup lime juice, fresh preferred♥
¼ cup diced tinned green chilies
1 small onion, finely chopped
2 medium tomatoes, peeled, seeded & chopped
3 tbsp. olive oil
1½ tsp. dried coriander leaves
1 tsp. salt
¼ tsp. dried oregano

Combine the fish & lime juice in a shallow dish. Cover & refrigerate, stirring occasionally until fish becomes opaque or ''cooked'', for **8 hours** or overnight. Combine the remaining ingredients. Stir into the fish & refrigerate, covered, at least **1 hour**. Serve with cocktail picks.

♥What to do with all those lime shells: They can be kept in a plastic bag for a couple of days in the refrigerator. Use for individual servings of Seviche as an appetizer before dinner or fill with scoops of icy sherbet for dessert. Don't forget to cut a slice from the bottom so they'll sit upright.

Salmon Mousse

A wonderfully delicate flavour & colour.

Yield: 1½ qt. capacity fancy mold or 9 × 5 inch loaf pan.

1 (7½ oz./220 g) tin red sockeye salmon, drained, bones & skin removed, mashed with a fork

2 tbsp. butter
2 tbsp. flour
1½ cups milk
1 slice of onion
6 peppercorns
Dash of mace or nutmeg
1 bay leaf
¾ cup mayonnaise

Salt & pepper to taste
1 envelope gelatin▾
¼ cup chicken stock or
   white wine▾▾
½ cup whipping cream,
   lightly whipped
1 tin medium shrimp,
rinsed & coarsely chopped

Place the milk, onion slice, peppercorns, mace or nutmeg & bay leaf in a small saucepan over medium-low heat for about **10 minutes**. Pour through a fine sieve into a small bowl. Discard the onion, peppercorns & bay leaf. In the same small saucepan, melt the butter, add the flour & cook about **2 minutes**. Add the milk gradually, stirring constantly to avoid lumps. Cook over medium heat, stirring until thickened & smooth. Remove from heat & cool slightly.

Combine the salmon & white sauce in a large bowl. Add the mayonnaise & season well with salt & freshly ground pepper. Set aside.

Sprinkle the gelatin over stock or wine in a small pan & let stand until spongy (about **5 minutes**). Dissolve over hot water. Stir into the salmon mixture along with the chopped shrimp. Chill in the refrigerator, stirring often to avoid lumping. When the mixture begins to set, fold in the lightly whipped cream. Taste & adjust the seasoning if necessary. Rinse the mold or pan with cold water. Do not dry. Pour the mixture into the mold or pan. Cover & chill until set. Unmold on a bed of greens. To serve, spread on slices of English cucumber or crackers. This can be prepared up to 2 days in advance.

▾If a firmer mousse is desired use 2 envelopes of gelatin.
▾▾Equal parts of dry white vermouth & water can be used as a substitute for white wine in most recipes.

House Scallops *(à la maison)*

For that continental touch.

Yield: About 2½ dozen.

½ cup butter
3 cups crumbs made from 3 to 4 English muffins
1 tbsp. finely chopped garlic
⅓ cup finely chopped parsley
¼ cup (approximately) clam juice♥
1 lb. scallops or halibut cut into 1 or 2 inch cubes
⅓ cup Parmesan cheese (freshly grated preferred)
2 tbsp. butter (reserve)

Melt ½ cup butter in pan over low heat. Add the crumbs &
garlic. Toss together about **3 to 6 minutes** or until crisp &
golden. Stir in the parsley. Spread about half of the mixture
into a buttered ovenproof serving dish approximately 9 ×
13 inches. Sprinkle with clam juice to moisten. Arrange the
scallops over the crumbs. Blend the remaining crumb
mixture with the cheese & spread on top. Dot with the 2
tbsp. butter, sprinkle with more clam juice & bake about
10 to 12 minutes at **450°F** until golden & tender. Serve
with cocktail picks. This may be prepared in individual
scallop dishes as an appetizer.

♥Clam juice comes in an 8 oz./250 mL bottle.

Corned Beef

Montreal & Winnipeg—move over!

Yield: About 10 lb. of deli-cious.

10 lb. brisket of beef
½ tin saltpetre (found in drugstores)
½ cup mixed pickling spice
½ cup pickling salt (coarse)
¼ cup brown sugar
4 cloves garlic, finely chopped

Mix all of the spices & cover the meat on both sides with them. Place in a glass pan. Cover with plastic wrap. Place the dish & all into a large plastic bag & close tightly so your entire refrigerator won't smell like a deli. Keep refrigerated for 5 days. Turn the meat at least twice during that time. On the sixth day, rinse well under the tap. Place in a large pan & cover with water. Bring to a simmer on top of the stove, then cover & put into a **325°F** oven for **6** to **8 hours** or until tender. Serve hot or cold, thinly sliced. This freezes well & the recipe can be halved successfully. Try this with one of our mustards on Page 81 through 83.

(On the seventh day, **rest**.)

A Duet of Kabobs

Colourful, unusual & yummy as an addition to any cocktail or buffet table.

Yield: About 4 dozen.

1 jar pickled watermelon rind
½ lb. cooked ham in a single piece
1 jar preserved kumquats
½ lb. smoked turkey in a single piece
Cocktail picks

Cut the meats & pickles in 1 inch pieces. Make the kabobs by combining the watermelon rind with the ham & the kumquats with the smoked turkey, or vice versa. Cover & refrigerate up to 1 day ahead.

Also good on kabobs are prosciutto, various salamis, kiwi fruit, peaches (fresh or tinned), mandarin oranges, pine-apple chunks, grapes, dried figs, etc.

Avocadobob: cut peeled avocado into bite-sized cubes. Dip in mayonnaise thinned with lemon juice. Roll in crushed corn or taco chips. Serve with cocktail picks.

Curried Meatballs

This doubles as a main course served with rice or noodles. Compliments will abound.

Yield: About 30 meatballs, depending on their size.

Meatballs:
1½ lb. lean ground beef or ground pork or a combination
1 cup fine dry bread crumbs
½ cup almonds, finely chopped
1 (8½ oz./227 g) tin water chestnuts, drained, rinsed & chopped
2 eggs
1 tbsp. soy sauce
2 cloves garlic, minced
1 tsp. salt
Cornstarch

Mix the meat with the bread crumbs, almonds, water chestnuts, eggs, soy sauce & garlic. Add the salt. Form balls about 1 inch in diameter. Roll in the cornstarch. Chill for several hours, then sauté in oil until the meat is cooked & the meatballs are nicely browned.

Or, place the meatballs in a large oiled roasting pan. Roast for approximately **25 minutes** at **350°F**, depending on the size of the meatballs. Check to make sure they are cooked through. These may be frozen. Thaw them before adding them to the sauce.

Sauce:

¾ cup sugar
¼ cup soy sauce
½ cup white vinegar
2 tbsp. cornstarch mixed with ½ cup water
1 tsp. grated ginger root or ½ tsp. dry ground ginger
2 tsp. curry powder
1 (19 oz./540 mL) tin pineapple chunks, drained, juice
   reserved

Mix the sugar, soy sauce, vinegar, cornstarch mixed with
water, ginger & curry powder in a saucepan. Add about
half of the reserved pineapple juice. Bring to a boil, stirring
constantly for **2** to **3 minutes** or until the mixture thinly
coats a spoon. Add the pineapple chunks & pour over the
meatballs. This can be made several days ahead &
refrigerated. When served, keep hot in a chafing dish.
Serve with cocktail picks.

Crunchy Baked Drumsticks

Great for an informal cocktail party.

Yield: About 20 drumsticks.

1 cup sour cream or plain yogurt
3 tbsp. lemon juice
1 clove garlic, minced
¼ tsp. Tabasco Sauce
1 tsp. salt
½ tsp. black pepper
2 cups toasted, fine bread crumbs♥
2 tsp. thyme
2 tsp. dry mustard
1 tsp. salt
1 tsp. paprika
¼ tsp. cayenne pepper
¼ tsp. black pepper
20 chicken drumsticks or thighs
½ cup melted butter

Mix together the sour cream, lemon juice, minced garlic clove, Tabasco, salt & pepper. Place the drumsticks in a large glass baking dish. Pour the marinade over the chicken pieces, making sure all are well covered. Cover with plastic wrap & marinate several hours or overnight.

Combine the rest of the ingredients. Roll the drumsticks in the crumb mixture, coating well. Shake to remove the excess. Place on buttered baking sheets & drizzle with melted butter. Bake in a preheated **375°F** oven for about **35 minutes** or until golden brown and tender. These are best served at room temperature or cold.

The drumsticks can be made 1 to 2 days ahead but they are best if made early on the day needed, covered loosely with a tea towel to retain their crunch & refrigerated. They are wonderful for picnics or lunch boxes.

Try different seasonings—perhaps rosemary, oregano, basil, marjoram, etc., or ½ cup grated Parmesan cheese added to the dry ingredients is very good.

♥It is important to toast the bread crumbs. Soda crackers or Melba toast may also be used but need not be toasted.

Chicken Wings Mahogany

Like no other chicken wing recipe you've tried. Outstanding!

Yield: 5 to 7 dozen, depending on the size of the wings.

1½ cups soy sauce
¾ cup dry sherry
1 cup hoisin sauce♥
¾ cup Chinese Plum Sauce♥
18 green onions, minced
6 large garlic cloves, minced
¾ cup cider vinegar
½ cup honey
1 tbsp. grated ginger root or 1 tsp. ground ginger
6 to 7 lb. chicken wings

In a 3 quart saucepan, combine all of the ingredients except the chicken wings. Bring to a boil & simmer **5 minutes**. Cool.

While the sauce is cooling, cut off the wing tips & set aside for making chicken stock. Place the wings in a large storage container. Pour the cooled sauce over the wings, cover & refrigerate overnight.

Place oven racks in the upper & lower thirds of the oven & preheat to **375°F**. Line 2 large shallow roasting pans with foil paper. Grease.

Drain the wings. Place on the prepared pans & bake uncovered **1 to 1½ hours**, basting about every **20 minutes** with the remaining sauce & turning to brown evenly. Be sure to switch the pans half-way through to assure even baking.

Remove the wings from the foil & place on fresh foil to cool. When cool, wrap & store for up to 3 days. Serve at room temperature.

You will have sauce left over. This keeps for weeks refrigerated. Try using it as a barbecue basting sauce.

♥Both of these products are available in Oriental food stores or gourmet shops, but do try the recipe for plum sauce, Page 81. It's delicious whenever you require this Oriental speciality!

Rye Whiskey Wieners

These are best prepared a day ahead.

Yield: About 40.

1 lb. cocktail wieners, cut into bite-sized pieces
½ cup rye whiskey
½ cup ketchup
½ cup brown sugar
Dash of Tabasco Sauce

Mix together the rye, ketchup, brown sugar & Tabasco Sauce. Add the wieners & simmer together about **40 minutes**. Serve hot from a chafing dish with cocktail picks.

These can be frozen.

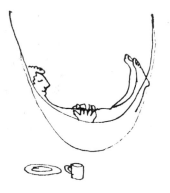

opposite:
Chicken Wings Mahogany, 71

Teriyaki Steak

This works as a main course as well, when served with rice.

Yield: About 30 kabobs (2 cubes of meat per kabob).

2 lb. sirloin steak, cut in 1 inch cubes
1 cup soy sauce
¼ cup dry sherry
¼ cup salad oil
½ cup minced onion
1 garlic clove, minced
1 tbsp. minced, fresh ginger root,
    or 1 tsp. ground ginger
1 (12 oz./341 mL) tin pineapple cubes, drained
    (reserve juice for another use)

Combine all of the ingredients, except the pineapple, in a large bowl. Cover & refrigerate, stirring occasionally, at least **4 hours** or overnight.

Remove from the marinade. Thread the meat cubes on skewers alternating them with pineapple cubes.

Broil & baste the kabobs with the marinade, turning as needed, **5 to 8 minutes**. (These can be made on a barbecue as well.) If wooden skewers are used, soak them for about **30 minutes** in water to prevent them from burning.

Country Pâté

This is an asset to a buffet table. Serve for lunch or take it on a picnic with French bread & one of our mustards.

Yield: 1 9 × 5 inch loaf.

1 lb. pork tenderloin	1 lb. coarsely ground pork
1 tbsp. clarified butter	1 lb. finely ground veal
½ tsp. salt	½ tsp. salt
Pinch pepper	Pinch of pepper, thyme
½ tsp. thyme	& allspice
¼ lb. chicken livers	¼ cup chopped fresh parsley
¼ cup Madeira wine♥	3 tbsp. heavy cream
¼ cup finely chopped green onions	2 eggs

Cut up the pork tenderloin into 1 inch chunks. Brown in a fry-pan over high heat, using the clarified butter. Season with the salt, pepper & thyme. Remove the pork & add the chicken livers, adding more butter if needed. Brown (cook only until pink inside) & season with salt & pepper. Remove the livers, turn off heat & add the wine & onions. Scrape up any bits clinging to the pan.

In a large bowl, place the ground pork & veal. Season with salt, pepper, thyme & allspice. Add the parsley, cream & eggs. Add the liver & pork mixture from the first group of ingredients. Mix well. Sauté 1 tbsp. of the mixture in order to taste for seasonings. Correct accordingly. Pack into a 9 × 5 inch loaf pan & place in a large pan with water approximately 1 inch deep. Cover the pâté tightly with foil & bake in a preheated **350°F** oven for **2½ hours** or until the fat & juices that have risen to the top are clear yellow. Remove the pâté from the oven & discard the foil.

Pour off the excess fat & let cool ½ **hour**. Loosely cover the mold with fresh foil & place a weight on top, e.g., a foil-covered brick. Refrigerate with the weight overnight. Unmold on a bed of greens & slice. Accompany with Eggplant & Olive Relish, Page 86, and sweet gherkins. This should be made at least **24 hours** or up to 3 days ahead.

♥Substitute for Madeira: 2 oz. red Burgundy wine plus 1 tbsp. cognac or brandy.

Clarified Butter

Melt any desired amount of butter (unsalted preferred) slowly over low heat in a heavy saucepan. When the last of the butter is melted, remove from the heat & carefully skim off the foam with a spoon. Strain the pure yellow oil through a paper-towel or cheese-cloth-lined sieve into a container, being certain to leave all the milky residue in the bottom of the pan. This pure oil, or ''clarified butter,'' may be stored in the freezer for months. Clarified butter is used to brown delicate meats such as veal, lamb or chicken quickly over very high heat. It has a high burning point & so it is less likely to burn.

Mini Dogs 'n Sauerkraut

Yield: About 40 minidogs.

These are a tasty novelty & perfect at a casual outdoor get-together.

The "Buns":
Make one recipe of Pâte à Choux, Page 48. Using a pastry bag fitted with a plain tip, pipe 3 inch éclairs onto lightly greased baking sheets. Brush with the egg glaze & bake as directed.

The Sauerkraut:
1 lb. sauerkraut, drained
1 onion, finely chopped
½ tsp. caraway seed
¼ cup butter
1½ cups dry white wine
2 tbsp. white wine vinegar
1 tbsp. sugar

Boil the drained sauerkraut in salted water for about **10 minutes**. Rinse under cold water, drain, then squeeze dry in a tea towel. Set aside.

In a large saucepan, sauté the onion & caraway seeds in the butter until soft. Add the sauerkraut, wine, vinegar, sugar; salt & pepper, to taste. Bring to a boil, then simmer, partially covered, stirring occasionally until most of the liquid has been absorbed (about **45 minutes**).

This can be prepared several days ahead. Reheat gently to serve.

The "Dogs":
About 2 lb. thin cocktail wieners or any long thin wiener of your choice.

Cut the wieners into 3 inch lengths. Put the prepared sauerkraut in a casserole dish, top with wieners, cover & bake in a preheated **350°F** oven for **20** to **30 minutes** or until heated through. (For a different flavour, do the wieners on the barbecue.)

The Mustard:
Prepare Sharp Dark Mustard, Page 82.

The Assembly:
Slit open a warmed éclair. Fill with about 1 tbsp.
sauerkraut, top with a wiener, dab with mustard & . . .
you know the rest!

Burger Bites

Yield: 1 dozen hearty servings.

1 lb. lean hamburger
¾ cup ketchup
1 tbsp. French-Style Mustard, Page 82,
    or Dijon mustard
2 tsp. Worcestershire sauce
1 cup chopped green pepper
1 cup chopped onion
¼ cup chopped parsley
1 tsp. salt
8 twists of freshly ground pepper
herbs to taste (choose from thyme, marjoram, oregano,
    basil or a combination thereof)

6 hamburger buns, split & lightly toasted or equivalent
    number of slices of French bread lightly toasted on
    one side

Mix the ingredients together until well blended. Spoon onto
the prepared buns or untoasted side of the French bread
slices. Place under a preheated broiler & broil until
done—about **6** to **7 minutes**, depending on how thick the
meat mixture is, so watch carefully. Slices of Cheddar or
Mozzarella or your favourite cheese may be melted on top
as well.

To freeze: Prepare as above to the cooking point, then
freeze on a baking sheet. When frozen, wrap well in plastic
wrap & foil for storage. Add some extra broiling time if
frozen.

Mama Mias

Yield: About 2 dozen.

8 oz./250 g Ricotta cheese
1 egg
¼ tsp. salt
4 oz. Mozzarella cheese, diced
4 slices salami, chopped
4 slices prosciutto, chopped♥
4 slices mortadella, chopped♥♥
½ cup freshly grated Parmesan cheese
freshly ground black pepper to taste

1 French stick, sliced & lightly toasted on one side or crusty rolls

Mix all of the ingredients together, combining well. Mound onto the untoasted side of the bread rounds. Freeze if desired. Place on a baking sheet & bake in a preheated **375°F** oven for about **10 minutes** or until hot & bubbly. If frozen, allow extra baking time.

♥Prosciutto is a cured Italian ham.
♥♥Mortadella is an Italian bologna.

Terrine of Chicken, Ham & Sausage with Cumberland Sauce

This is a great addition to a cocktail buffet table or a luncheon. It's also great as an appetizer. Serve with Cumberland Sauce, Page OO.

Yield: One 11½ × 4½ inch loaf.

3 to 4 cups cooked chicken
1 lb. pork sausage meat, uncooked
½ lb. diced boiled ham
3 cloves garlic, finely chopped
2 eggs, slightly beaten
1 tsp. thyme
3 tbsp. chopped fresh parsley
¼ cup brandy or chicken stock
½ tsp. salt
½ tsp. pepper
½ cup butter, softened
½ lb. sliced, uncooked bacon

Chop the chicken into medium-size pieces. Set aside.

In a large bowl, mix together the sausage, ham, garlic, eggs, thyme, parsley, brandy, salt, pepper & butter.

Line a loaf pan (we used an 11½ × 4½ inch pan, but a 9 × 5 inch loaf pan is great too) with uncooked bacon. Cover with ⅓ of the sausage meat mixture; top with half of the chicken. Continue layering, ending with sausage. Top with bacon slices. Cover with foil. Place the terrine in a hot water bath. (We used a roaster, with 1 inch of water.) Bake at **350°F** about **1½ hours**, or until the juices run clear. Add more boiling water to the roaster if needed. Remove from the water bath. Drain off the fat. Let the terrine stand **1 hour**. Remove the foil. Cover with fresh foil & weight the terrine with 2 or 3 cans of food. (We used a brick covered with foil.) Chill overnight. This is best made 2 or 3 days ahead. Serve on a bed of parsley or watercress or lettuce leaves. This slices beautifully as you can see in the photograph opposite Page 80.

♥Sauté some of sausage mixture in order to taste for seasoning. Adjust accordingly.

Home-Made Condiments

Cumberland Sauce

Cumberland sauce can be served hot or cold. It's great with chicken or ham & definitely fantastic with the chicken & ham terrine.

Yield: About 2½ cups.

1 cup red currant jelly
½ cup fresh orange juice
½ tsp. dry mustard
¼ tsp. powdered ginger
Zest˅ of 1 orange & 1 lemon, cut in thin strips
1 cup port wine

Blanch the orange & lemon peels in boiling water about **5 minutes;** drain & rinse. (This helps to get rid of any bitterness in the peel.)

Put all of the ingredients in a saucepan & cook over low heat, stirring constantly, until the jelly melts. This keeps for weeks in the refrigerator.

˅ For definition of "zest", see Page 13.

Try This: Preheat the broiler. Place 24 chicken wings (tips removed) on a foil-lined baking sheet. Sprinkle with salt & pepper. Broil **5 minutes** each side. Remove from the broiler. Set oven at **400°F**. Baste the wings with Cumberland Sauce & bake about **½ hour**, turning & basting 3 or 4 times. Serve hot or cold. Deeelish!

opposite:
Terrine of Chicken, Ham & Sausage, 79
with Cumberland Sauce, 80

Plum Sauce

1 cup plum jam
½ cup chutney (hot mango is very good)
1 tbsp. vinegar
¼ tsp. Tabasco Sauce

Combine the ingredients in a saucepan. Cook over medium
heat until thoroughly blended & bubbling. Pour into a
sterilized jar & cap tightly. Store in the refrigerator.

Home-Made Mustards

Banish the ball park mustard from your life! Try these.
They keep very well in tightly sealed containers in the
refrigerator. They make excellent gifts from the kitchen &
men love them.

Green Peppercorn Mustard

Yield: About 1 cup.

Make the French-Style Mustard on Page 82, letting it cool
for **5 minutes**. Stir in 4 tsp. drained, rinsed & crushed
green peppercorns.

To keep an opened jar of mustard fresh longer, put a slice of
lemon or lime on top & reseal.

A French-Style Mustard

Yield: About 1 cup.

⅓ cup dry English mustard
1 tbsp. sugar
¼ tsp. salt
2 eggs, beaten
⅔ cup tarragon vinegar

In a small saucepan, combine the mustard, sugar & salt. Combine the eggs with the vinegar & add slowly to the dry mixture, stirring constantly. Cook the mixture over moderate heat, continuing to stir until it is thickened & smooth. Let the mustard cool.

Pour into a jar & refrigerate.

Sharp Dark Mustard

Yield: About 1 cup.

1 cup cider vinegar
4 whole cloves
4 black peppercorns
2 small bay leaves
¼ tsp. salt
1 cup dry English mustard
¼ cup sugar

Combine the vinegar, cloves, peppercorns, bay leaves & salt in a small saucepan. Bring to a boil over medium heat. Reduce the heat & simmer **5 minutes**. Strain into a small bowl. In another bowl, combine the mustard & sugar. Add the vinegar mixture gradually, stirring constantly. Beat until smooth. Pour into a jar & refrigerate.

Tangy Sweet Mustard

Yield: About 1½ cups.

½ cup dry English mustard
¼ cup white sugar
⅛ tsp. salt
2 eggs, beaten
½ cup cider vinegar
½ cup water
2 tbsp. butter

Mix the dry mustard, sugar & salt in a small saucepan. Beat the vinegar, eggs & water together in a small bowl. Add slowly to the dry ingredients in the saucepan, stirring to avoid lumps. Cook the mixture over medium heat until thick & smooth. Remove from heat. Add the butter in bits, stirring to incorporate well. Cool. Pour into jars & refrigerate.

Blender Mayonnaise

Yield: About 1½ cups.

This is the easiest & best mayonnaise you could hope for. Just be sure the egg, oil & lemon juice are at room temperature before you begin. Add the oil *very slowly* until about one half is used & the sauce thickens into a heavy cream. After this stage, more oil may be added with greater speed.

¼ **cup olive oil**
1 egg
1 tsp. dry mustard
½ tsp. salt
dash of cayenne pepper
¾ to 1 cup salad oil
2 tbsp. lemon juice

Combine the ¼ cup olive oil, egg, mustard, salt & cayenne in a blender or food processor. With the machine running, add the salad oil **very slowly** in a **slow steady stream**. When about ⅔ of the oil has been incorporated, add the lemon juice. Check the consistency—when the mixture is creamy & thick—**STOP!** If it is too thick, add more oil until the desired consistency is achieved. Voilà!

This will keep (tightly covered) in the refrigerator for about 2 weeks. You may find that the mayonnaise thickens quite a bit on standing. If so, thin with a little cream.

Celery & Olive Relish

Put some crunch in your life.

Yield: About 2 cups.

2 cups diced celery, including some leaves
2 tbsp. finely chopped olives with pimiento
1 tsp. oregano
1 tbsp. salad oil
1 tbsp. white vinegar
Salt & pepper to taste

Combine all of the ingredients, cover & refrigerate for at least 4 hours. This keeps for several days in the refrigerator.

With some mayonnaise to bind it (1 to 2 tbsp.), this makes a good filling for cherry tomatoes or pâte à choux.

Martini Olives: Offer a generous bowl of green olives marinated in gin.

Eggplant-Olive Relish

This keeps for several days in the refrigerator & indeed improves with age (but, then, don't we all?).

Yield: About 1 quart.

1 small eggplant
2 medium green peppers, roughly chopped
3 tbsp. olive oil
3 tbsp. wine vinegar (unflavoured)
1 large tomato, peeled, seeded & chopped
2 to 3 tbsp. finely chopped parsley
1 clove garlic, minced
1 cup pitted ripe olives, coarsely chopped
Salt & pepper to taste

Peel the eggplant & cut it into 1 inch cubes. Sprinkle it with salt. This helps rid the eggplant of excess moisture & any bitterness. Place the eggplant in a colander & let it stand **20** to **30 minutes**. Rinse well under cold water & pat dry with paper towels. Steam until soft. Allow to cool.

Place the cut peppers, eggplant, tomato & parsley in a food processor & with a quick on-off motion chop roughly (you don't want this too mushy). Add the rest of the ingredients & give the mixture a couple of very quick on-offs. Add salt & pepper to taste. Serve with buttered French bread or pita bread.

Try this on hamburgers or hot dogs—it's delicious!

An Experience: a bowl of cherry tomatoes, a bowl of vodka, a bowl of coarse salt. Dip the tomatoes in vodka, then in the coarse salt. Heaven!

Sweet Indulgence

Send them home with coffee & . .

Almond Butter Cake

Terrific with cheese, fruit & wine.

Yield: 1 9 inch cake.

1¼ cups butter, softened
¾ cup sugar
½ tsp. salt
1 egg
2 egg yolks
⅓ cup ground blanched almonds♥
2 tsp. kirsch or ½ tsp. almond extract
1½ tsp. vanilla
1¾ cups all-purpose flour, sifted
1 egg, lightly beaten
Powdered sugar

Preheat the oven to **350°F**. Butter a 9 × 1½ inch fluted tart pan with a removable bottom, or a 9 inch cake tin. Beat the butter, sugar & salt in a large mixer bowl until light & fluffy. Beat in 1 egg & the egg yolks, one at a time, beating well after each addition. Beat in the almonds, kirsch & vanilla. Fold in the flour, mixing well. Spoon the batter into the prepared tart pan. Spread evenly. Brush with the beaten egg. Bake until the top is golden, about **30 minutes**. Cool in the pan on a wire rack. Dust lightly with powdered sugar. This is better made a day ahead & stored, covered, at room temperature.

♥For a different flavour, try roasting whole blanched almonds or other nuts. Grind & measure.

How to make your own vanilla extract:

2 split vanilla beans
1 cup brandy or vodka

Place the vanilla beans in a sterile glass jar. Pour liquor over them, cover & let stand in a cool dark place for at least one month. This makes a great gift from the kitchen.

Almond Roca Bars

Yield: About 4 dozen.

1 cup firmly packed brown sugar
1 cup butter
1 small box graham wafers (about 40)
3 85 g Hershey chocolate bars
1 cup almonds, toasted & ground

Line a 10½ × 15½ inch rimmed baking sheet with whole
graham wafers (the entire surface won't be covered).
Combine butter & brown sugar in a heavy saucepan &
cook over medium heat for **5 minutes**. The mixture has a
tendency to separate, so make sure you stir with gusto.
Pour over the graham wafers. Place the chocolate bars on
top immediately so that the heat from the caramel will melt
them. Working quickly, spread the chocolate over all.
Sprinkle with toasted almonds. Cool. Cut in squares. These
freeze perfectly.

You may have to pop the pan into a **200°F** oven for a few
minutes to help with melting the chocolate.

Ice Cream Cookies

By hand or in a food processor, these are quick & easy to make.

Yield: Makes about 3 dozen, depending on their size.

⅔ **cup butter**
⅔ **cup icing sugar**
2 beaten egg yolks
2 tsp. vanilla
2 cups all-purpose flour

Preheat the oven to **350°F**. Cream the butter & sugar thoroughly. Add the egg yolks & vanilla. Beat well. Add the flour & roll into a ball. Break off small amounts & roll in your hands to form small balls. Place on an ungreased baking sheet & press with fork tines. (A potato masher makes a good impression.) Bake **15** to **20 minutes** or until lightly browned.

Icing Sugar Substitute: 1 cup white sugar, 1 tbsp. cornstarch. Put in a blender or food processor. Mix until it no longer feels grainy.

Lemon Cheese Fingers

Yield: About 8 dozen.

1 cup sugar
1 cup butter, softened
4 oz./125 g plain cream cheese, softened
1 egg yolk
2½ cups all-purpose flour
1 cup finely chopped walnuts
½ tsp. salt
zest of ½ lemon♥
1 (6 oz./175 g) package semi-sweet chocolate chips, melted
Chocolate decorating sprinkles

Cream the butter, sugar & cream cheese in a large mixer bowl until light & fluffy. Beat in the egg yolk & stir in the flour, walnuts & lemon zest. Refrigerate, covered, at least 2 hours. Heat oven to **325°F**. Shape about 1 tbsp. of the dough into a 1 inch log. Repeat until all the dough is used. Place on ungreased baking sheets. Bake until light brown —about **12 minutes**. Cool on wire racks. Dip the ends of the logs in chocolate, then into chocolate sprinkles. Let stand until the chocolate sets. Store them between layers of waxed paper in cookie tins. Freeze no longer than 3 months.

♥For a definition of ''zest'', see Page 13.

Millionaire Bars

For all of you out there who have been after this recipe for years—here it is!

Yield: About 7 dozen, depending on their size.

1 cup margarine
½ cup sugar
2 cups all-purpose flour
1 tin Eagle Brand Milk
⅔ cup sugar
4 tbsp. corn syrup
1 cup margarine
3 85 g Jersey Milk chocolate bars

Preheat oven to **375°F**. If a glass baking dish is used, reduce the temperature by **25°F**.

Cream the margarine & ½ cup sugar. Add the flour. Mix until smooth. Press evenly into a 9 × 13 inch pan. Bake at **375°F** for **25 to 30 minutes**. Watch carefully to avoid over-browning. Cool.

In a heavy saucepan, combine the Eagle Brand Milk, ⅔ cup sugar, corn syrup & margarine. Bring to a boil over medium heat, stirring constantly to avoid burning. Cook **5 minutes**. (If some browning occurs, strain the mixture through a fine sieve to remove any brown particles.) Remove from heat. Pour over the cookie base while still hot. Top with the chocolate bars. Allow the chocolate to melt; then spread over the filling. If the chocolate doesn't melt sufficiently, put the pan into a warm (about **200°F**) oven for **2 to 3 minutes**. Cool to allow to set. Cut in squares with a warm knife. These can be frozen.

Sesame Seed Cookies

Yield: About 4 dozen, depending on their size.

2 cups all-purpose flour
¾ cup sugar
1½ tsp. baking powder
¼ tsp. salt
⅔ cup shortening
2 egg yolks
¼ cup milk
1 tsp. vanilla
⅓ cup sesame seeds

Preheat oven to **375°F**. Grease baking sheets. Sift the dry ingredients into a bowl. Cut in the shortening with a pastry blender until the mixture resembles coarse crumbs. Add the egg yolks, milk & vanilla. Mix until the dough holds together. Knead until smooth. Shape rounded tablespoonsful into ovals. Roll in the sesame seeds. Bake at **375°F** for **15 to 20 minutes** or until brown. These can be frozen.

You can also use an electric mixer or food processor 'cause then you don't need to knead.

Short of eggs? One whole egg will substitute for 2 egg yolks.

A substitute for 1 tsp. baking powder: ½ tsp. cream of tartar & ¼ tsp. baking soda.

Spice Cookies

Great with a cup of tea—far out with cappucino.

Yield: About 3½ dozen.

½ cup butter
½ cup firmly packed brown sugar♥
1¼ cups all-purpose flour
½ tsp. ginger
¼ tsp. cinnamon
½ tsp. allspice
½ tsp. baking powder
¼ cup almonds, finely chopped

Cream the butter & sugar together. Sift together the dry
ingredients. Add them to the creamed mixture & mix well.
Add the chopped almonds. Shape into two long rolls. Wrap
in lightly buttered foil & refrigerate or freeze. Cut into
½ inch slices. Bake in preheated **400°F** oven **5** to
7 minutes or until nicely browned.

♥*Brown sugar substitute:* 2 tbsp. dark molasses, 1 cup white sugar. Stir
together or place in a blender & blend until well mixed.

Punches & Coolers

A Bar Guide for About 25 Guests

15 lb. ice for drinks
2 bottles vodka
1 bottle gin
2 bottles scotch
2 bottles rye
2 bottles special wines—sherry or Dubonnet
6 bottles white wine
16 to 20 large bottles club soda, tonic, ginger ale, diet
     pop & mineral waters
Orange juice & V-8 or tomato juice if screwdrivers or
     Bloody Marys are to your liking.

Keep the bar as simple as possible. Make sure there is
plenty of ice. Slices of fresh orange, lemon or lime give a
nice touch. Place the bar in a location away from the flow of
things so people can circulate easily. Don't forget the non-
drinkers in the crowd.

The expression ''to drink a toast'' dates from Victorian England, when
slices of toast were added to the wassail bowl.

Mixing Drinks & Hors-d'oeuvres

Mixed Drinks: Serve zippy, tangy, highly seasoned hors-d'oeuvres.

White Wine: Nothing too highly seasoned is needed, but almost anything else goes well.

Champagne: Don't get too gutsy; keep the flavours simple. Caviar on thin toast strips is wonderful. (Simple, eh!)

Bengal Lancers' Punch

Yield: About 45 4-oz. cups.

1 26 oz. white rum
1 26 oz. vodka
3 26 oz. dry white wine
½ bottle daiquiri mix
13 oz. Triple Sec
1 large (1 litre) bottle ginger ale

Fill a ring mold with freshly boiled, cooled water. Freeze. Mix all of the well-chilled liquids except the ginger ale in advance & rebottle in empty liquor & wine bottles. Refrigerate. This allows for the "perfect marriage" of ingredients. Use a bottle or two at a time as needed, adding ginger ale accordingly. To serve, place the ice ring in a punch bowl; add the liquors & ginger ale. Wow! Plan to serve lots of coffee after this one.

Wondering what to do with leftover celery leaves? The Ancient Romans wore wreaths of celery leaves on their heads as a cure for The Morning After the Night Before. (Please let us know if this works.)

To make crystal-clear ice cubes: boil water, let it cool & pour it into ice cube trays.

Hot Buttered Rum

A warm welcome for guests on a cold night.

Yield: About 10 drinks.

½ cup butter
½ cup firmly packed brown sugar
½ tsp cinnamon
½ tsp. nutmeg
¼ tsp. ground cloves
Pinch of salt

Mix the butter & sugar till light & fluffy. Add the remaining ingredients & mix well. Store in a covered jar. To serve, combine 2 tsp. of the mix with 2 oz. dark rum in a mug. Fill with hot water. Super as a gift from the kitchen.

Kir

A refreshing aperitif.

Yield: 1 serving.

1 part crème de cassis
4 to 5 parts dry white wine, chilled

Serve over ice if desired.

Margaritas

Oh what a Señorita!

Yield: Serves about 6.

1 (6 oz./178 mL) tin frozen limeade
6 oz. tequila
2 oz. Triple Sec
Lemon or lime juice
Salt

Dip the rims of the glasses into lime juice & then into salt. Set aside. Fill a blender ¾ full with ice cubes. Add the limeade, tequila & Triple Sec. Blend well & pour into the prepared glasses.

Pink Sours

Yield: Serves about 6.

1 (6 oz./178 mL) tin frozen pink lemonade
1 lemonade can filled with beer
6 to 8 oz. whiskey
3 large ice cubes

Combine the above ingredients in a blender. Pour over crushed ice. Garnish with orange slices & maraschino cherries.

A Cooler

Yield: 1 serving.

1½ oz. Ruby Port
Ice cubes
Club soda

Pour the Ruby Port over ice. Fill the glass with club soda. Garnish with a slice of lemon.

Sangria

Yield: About 1½ quarts.

1 lemon, sliced
1 lime, sliced
1 orange, sliced
4 oz. brandy
¼ cup sugar
1 26 oz. bottle Spanish red wine
2 tbsp. lemon juice, or to taste
Club soda

In a large glass pitcher, combine the brandy & sugar. Add the prepared fruits. Let stand at room temperature **1 hour**. Add the wine & lemon juice & let stand at room temperature for another hour. Just before serving, add ice cubes & fill the pitcher with club soda. Stir well.

Make ice cubes out of club soda if you like.

Ice Cube Variations: Place a strawberry, grape, raspberry, peach slice, orange segment or whatever in each compartment of an ice tray. Fill with water & freeze. Use with white wine, white grape juice or other fruit drinks.

Try cranberry juice & club soda over ice with a couple of banana slices.

White Sangria

Yield: About 1½ quarts.

1 26 oz. bottle dry white wine, chilled
5 tbsp. orange-flavoured liqueur
2 cups chilled club soda
1 apple, cored & sliced
1 orange, sliced
½ lemon, sliced

In a large glass pitcher, combine the wine & liqueur. Stir in the club soda & add the prepared fruits. Serve over ice.

White Grape Punch

This is the best non-alcoholic punch we've tasted.

Yield: About 4 quarts or 32 ½ cup servings.

3 24 oz. or 2¼ 1 L bottles white grape juice, chilled
1 28 oz. or 1 L bottle club soda, chilled
1 pint fresh strawberries, hulled
   or small jar maraschino cherries, drained
1 small tin sliced cling peaches, chilled & drained,
   juice reserved
1 small tin sliced pears, chilled & drained, juice reserved
1 large lemon, thinly sliced
1 small tin pineapple chunks, chilled & drained,
   juice reserved
1 tbsp. aromatic bitters (Angostura Bitters)

Large ice ring or see suggestion below.

In a 6 quart chilled punch bowl, combine all of the ingredients.

To serve, ladle the juice mixture with some fruit into glasses. Use cocktail picks to rescue the fruit.

We arrange the fruits in a large muffin pan, fill with reserved fruit juices & freeze. This gives you flavoured ice cubes & doesn't dilute the punch as will ice cubes made with water.

"The Nuts"

Iced Almonds

Great gift from the kitchen.

Yield: About 2 cups.

1 cup whole blanched almonds
½ cup sugar
2 tbsp. butter or margarine
½ tsp. vanilla
¾ tsp. salt

Butter a large sheet of foil. Heat the almonds, sugar &
butter over medium heat in a heavy fry-pan, stirring constantly until the almonds are toasted & the sugar is golden
brown—at least **15 minutes**, so be patient.♥ Remove from
heat, stir in the vanilla, spread the nuts on the buttered
foil & sprinkle with salt. Cool. Break into clusters.

♥You will note three distinct stages. The mixture:

1. liquifies (butter & sugar melt)
2. crystallizes (turns white & chunks)
3. liquifies again & starts to caramelize.

Nuts & Bolts

Yield: About 32 cups.

2 lb. mixed nuts
8 cups pretzel sticks
8 cups Shreddies
8 cups Cheerios
4 cups chow mein noodles
1 cup salad oil
1 cup melted butter or margarine
2 tbsp. Worcestershire sauce
1 tbsp. garlic salt
1 tbsp. seasoned salt

Pour all of the dry ingredients into a large roasting pan.
Pour the oil & melted butter & the rest of the seasonings
over top & mix well. Bake in a preheated **275°F** oven **30** to
45 minutes, stirring every **15 minutes** until heated through
& nice & toasty. These can be frozen.

Sugared Peanuts

Every cocktail party needs a few nuts.

Yield: 2 cups.

2 cups raw peanuts
1 cup sugar
½ cup water
salt

In a heavy saucepan, combine the peanuts, sugar & water.
Cook & stir until the sugar crystallizes & coats the peanuts
(about **10 minutes**).

Spread the peanuts on a buttered 15½ × 10½ inch baking
sheet. Sprinkle with salt. Bake in a **300°F** oven for
15 minutes, stirring once or twice. Continue baking
15 minutes more or until nicely browned. Remove from
the pan, cool & store in a non-plastic container.

Toasted Nut & Dried Fruit Mix

This is soooooo good!

Yield: About 7 or 8 cups.

1½ cups raw almonds
1½ cups raw cashews
1½ cups raw peanuts
3 tbsp. melted butter
½ lb. dried apricots, cut in quarters with wet scissors
3 cups dark & light raisins, mixed
Salt

Combine the nuts. Add the melted butter, mixing well. Place on a baking sheet & bake in a preheated **350°F** oven for **15** to **20 minutes** or until golden. Stir a few times. Remove from the oven. Sprinkle with salt. Add the dried fruits. Mix well. Let cool.

This can be made days in advance & stored in the refrigerator, but do not add the apricots or raisins until just before serving. Serve at room temperature.

Menu Suggestions

Please have fun with these.
Try any or all, mix & match, or add to, but above
all—enjoy!

A Children's Birthday Party

Crudité of raw vegetables with the
Curry Vegetable Dipping Sauce
Baked Cheese Puffs
Crunchy Baked Drumsticks with paper frills
Chocolate milk
Birthday cake & ice cream
or
Oversized chocolate chip cookies
(decorate with a goodly dollop of
icing in the centre to plant a candle in)

Poker Night

Toasted Nut & Dried Fruit Mix
Corned Beef & Mustards
Assorted rye breads
Duet of Kabobs
Cheese tray & crackers
Fat dill pickles
Sesame Seed Cookies
Domestic & imported beers
Coffee

After Theatre

Hot Anchovy-Flavoured Dip
French bread & basket of vegetables
Red wine
Assorted cheeses & crackers
Bowl of dried fruits & nuts
A little something for the sweet tooth

When the Ladies Get Together

Kir
Pâte à Choux with assorted fillings
Crudité of fresh vegetables
Roquefort Cheese Dip
Pickles & olives
Orange Cream Cheese Ball with digestive biscuits
Generous bowl of icy cold seedless grapes
Lemon Cheese Fingers

Sunday Afternoon at Home

Camembert Cream—assorted crackers
Terrine of Chicken, Ham & Sausage
with Cumberland Sauce
Spinach Tart
Relish tray
Iced Almonds or Sugared Peanuts
Fruit cake
or
Almond Butter Cake
Steaming cups of tea

The Cocktail Buffet

Toasted Nut & Dried Fruit Mix
Gruyère Shortbread
Antipasto with Deep-Fried Shells
Spicy Hot Shrimp Dip with ripple chips
Ginger Roll
Cheese Swirls
Mushroom Turnovers
Curried Meatballs
Salmon Mousse with cucumber slices
Variety of cold cuts, breads & mustards
Large bowls of olives & gherkins
Cheese, fresh & dried fruits
Millionaire Bars, etc.

Having a Bunch for Brunch

Bloody Marys or champagne & orange juice
Fresh fruits
Mushroom Tart
Celery stuffed with Hot Crab Dip
Platter of sliced tomatoes
Your favourite coffee cake, muffins or Danish
Gallons of coffee

Al Fresco (Outdoor) Gathering

Hot Cheese Dip with Tortilla Chips
Crudité of fresh vegetables
Chili Doughnuts with Guacamole Sauce
Seviche
A generous bowl of chilled melon balls
(watermelon, honeydew, cantaloupe, etc.)
Almond Roca Bars
Margaritas or Sangria or beer

Metric Conversion Guideline

For translating your recipes to metric:

¼ teaspoon	⇔	1 mL
½ teaspoon	⇔	2 mL
1 teaspoon	⇔	5 mL
1 tablespoon	⇔	15 mL
¼ cup	⇔	50 mL
⅓ cup	⇔	75 mL
½ cup	⇔	125 mL
⅔ cup	⇔	150 mL
¾ cup	⇔	175 mL
1 cup	⇔	250 mL

Replace

1 oz.	⇔	25 g
4 oz./¼ lb.	⇔	125 g
8 oz./½ lb.	⇔	250 g
16 oz./1 lb.	⇔	500 g
2 lb.	⇔	1 kg

Index

A Cooler, 98
Advice, 8-9
Almond Butter Cake, 87
Almond Roca Bars, 88
Antipasto, 16
Avocado & Salmon Filling, 27

Bacon & Gruyère Filling, 34
Baked Cheese Puffs, 57
Bar Guide, 94
Basic Pastry for Savouries, 36
Bengal Lancers' Punch, 95
Black Olive Spread, 10
Blender Mayonnaise, 84
Burger Bites, 77

Camembert Cream, 11
Celery & Olive Relish, 85
Cheddar-Cashew Filling, 34
CHEESE
    Bacon & Gruyère Filling, 34
    Baked Cheese Puffs, 57
    Black Olive Spread, 10
    Camembert Cream, 11
    Cheddar-Cashew Filling, 34
    Cheese Swirls, 56
    Cheese Tarts, 43
    Christmas Eve Chip Dip, 12
    Cream Cheese Pastry, 37
    Feta Cream, 13
    Gouda Shrimp Balls, 50
    Gruyère Shortbread, 53
    Herb Cheese, 20
    Herbed Gougère, 49
    Hot Cheese Dip, 21
    Indonesian Cream, 14
    Lemon Cheese Fingers, 90
    Mama Mias, 78
    Mozzarella & Anchovy Filling, 35
    Niçoise-Style Filling, 34
    Onion Wafers, 54
    Orange Cream Cheese, 13
    Roquefort Cheese Dip, 24
    Spicy Hot Shrimp Dip, 23
    Spinach Tart, 42
    Stilton Wafers, 55
    Stuffed Cucumber Cups, 45
    Swiss Cheese Stacks, 14
    We'll Name It Later Spread, 25
    Whole Wheat Cheddar Hearts, 54
Cheese Swirls, 56
Cheese Tarts, 43
CHICKEN
    Chicken Wings Mahogany, 71
    Chutney Chicken Puffs, 46
    Crunchy Baked Drumsticks, 70
    Curried Almond Chicken Filling, 29
    Terrine of Chicken, Ham & Sausage, 79
Chicken Wings Mahogany, 71
Chili Doughnuts, 47
Christmas Eve Chip Dip, 12
Chutney Chicken Puffs, 46
Clam Filling, 33
Clarified Butter, 75
Cocktail Biscuits, 51
CONDIMENTS
    Blender Mayonnaise, 84
    Celery & Olive Relish, 85
    Cumberland Sauce, 80
    Eggplant & Olive Relish, 86
    French-Style Mustard, 82
    Green Peppercorn Mustard, 81
    Martini Olives, 85
    Plum Sauce, 81
    Sharp Dark Mustard, 82
    Tangy Sweet Mustard, 83
Corned Beef, 66
Corned Beef & Green Pepper Filling, 28
Country Pâté, 74
Cream Cheese Pastry, 37
Crunchy Baked Drumsticks, 70
Cumberland Sauce, 80
Curried Almond Chicken Filling, 29
Curried Meatballs, 68
Curry Vegetable Dipping Sauce, 26

Deep Fried Pasta Shells, 59
DIPS
  Antipasto, 16
  Christmas Eve Chip Dip, 12
  Curry Vegetable Dipping Sauce,
    26
  Guacamole Sauce, 17
  Hot Anchovy-Flavoured, 19
  Hot Cheese, 21
  Hot Crab, 22
  Roquefort Cheese, 24
  Spicy Hot Shrimp, 23
Duet of Kabobs, 67

Eggplant & Olive Relish, 86

Feta Cream, 13
FILLINGS
  Avocado & Salmon, 27
  Bacon & Gruyère, 34
  Black Olive, 10
  Celery & Olive Relish, 85
  Cheddar-Cashew, 34
  Cheese Swirls, 56
  Clam, 33
  Corned Beef & Green Pepper,
    28
  Curried Almond Chicken, 29
  Herb Cheese, 20
  Hot Crab, 22
  Mozzarella & Anchovy, 35
  Mushroom, 39
  Mustard Stuffed Eggs, 30
  Niçoise-Style, 34
  Smoked Salmon Stuffed Eggs,
    31
  Spinach, 35
  Tuna & Caper, 32
  We'll Name It Later, 25
FISH
  Antipasto, 16
  Avocado & Salmon, 27
  Cheese Swirls, 56
  Clam, 33
  Ginger Roll, 38
  Gouda Shrimp Balls, 50
  Hot Anchovy-Flavoured Dip, 19

  Hot Crab Dip, 22
  House Scallops, 65
  Mozzarella & Anchovy, 35
  Salmon Mousse, 64
  Sardine Fingers, 40
  Seviche, 63
  Shrimp & Red Onion Spread, 15
  Smoked Salmon Stuffed Eggs,
    31
  Spicy Hot Shrimp, 23
  Stuffed Cucumber Cups, 45
  Tuna & Caper, 32
French-Style Mustard, 82

Ginger Roll, 38
Gouda Shrimp Balls, 50
Green Peppercorn Mustard, 81
Gruyère Shortbread, 53
Guacamole Sauce, 17

Herb Cheese, 20
Herbed Gougère, 49
Hot Anchovy-Flavoured Dip, 19
Hot Buttered Rum, 96
Hot Cheese Dip, 21
Hot Crab Dip, 22
House Scallops, 65

Ice Cream Cookies, 89
Iced Almonds, 100
Indonesian Cream, 14

Kir, 96

Lemon Cheese Fingers, 90

Mama Mias, 78
Margaritas, 97
Mayonnaise, 84
MEAT
  Bacon & Gruyère, 34
  Burger Bites, 77
  Chili Doughnuts, 47
  Cocktail Biscuits, 51
  Corned Beef, 66
  Corned Beef & Green Pepper,
    28

110

Country Pâté, 74
Curried Meatballs, 68
Duet of Kabobs, 67
Ginger Roll, 38
Mama Mias, 78
Mini Dogs 'n Sauerkraut, 76
Rye Whiskey Wieners, 72
Teriyaki Steak, 73
Terrine of Chicken, Ham &
   Sausage, 79
We'll Name It Later Spread, 25
Mediterranean Pastries, 44
MENU SUGGESTIONS
   A Children's Birthday Party, 103
   After-Theatre, 104
   Alfresco (Outdoor) Gathering,
   107
   Having a Bunch for Brunch, 107
   Poker Night, 104
   Sunday Afternoon at Home, 105
   The Cocktail Buffet, 106
   When the Ladies Get Together,
   105
Metric Conversion Guideline, 108
Millionaire Bars, 91
Mini Dogs 'n Sauerkraut, 76
Mini Omelettes, 61
Mozzarella & Anchovy Filling, 35
Mushroom Tart, 41
Mushroom Turnovers, 39
MUSTARDS
   French-Style, 82
   Green Peppercorn, 81
   Sharp Dark, 82
   Tangy Sweet, 83
Mustard Stuffed Eggs, 30

Niçoise-Style Filling, 34
NUTS
   Iced Almonds, 100
   Nuts & Bolts, 101
   Sugared Peanuts, 101
   Toasted Nut & Dried Fruit
   Mix, 102
Nuts & Bolts, 101

Onion Wafers, 54

Orange Cream Cheese, 13
PASTRY
   Basic Pastry for Savouries, 36
   Cheese Tarts, 43
   Chutney Chicken Puffs, 46
   Cream Cheese Pastry, 37
   Ginger Roll, 38
   Gouda Shrimp Balls, 50
   Herbed Gougère, 49
   Mediterranean Pastries, 44
   Mini Dogs 'n Sauerkraut, 76
   Mushroom Tart, 41
   Mushroom Turnovers, 39
   Pâte à Choux, 48
   Sardine Fingers, 40
Pâte Brisée, 36
Pâte à Choux, 48
Pink Sours, 97
Plum Sauce, 81
PUNCHES & COOLERS
   A Cooler, 98
   Bengal Lancers' Punch, 95
   Hot Buttered Rum, 96
   Kir, 96
   Margaritas, 97
   Pink Sours, 97
   Sangria, 98
   White Grape Punch, 99
   White Sangria, 99

Roquefort Cheese Dip, 24
Rye Whiskey Wieners, 72

Salmon Mousse, 64
Sangria, 98
Sardine Fingers, 40
SAUCES
   Cumberland, 80
   Curry Vegetable, 26
   Guacamole, 17
   Plum, 81
Sesame Seed Cookies, 92
Seviche, 63
Sharp Dark Mustard, 82
Shrimp & Red Onion Spread, 15
Smoked Salmon Stuffed Eggs, 31

Spice Cookies, 93
Spicy Hot Shrimp Dip, 23
Spinach Filling, 35
Spinach Pâté, 60
Spinach Tart, 42
SPREADS
  Black Olive, 10
  Camembert Cream, 11
  Cheese Swirls, 56
  Eggplant & Olive Relish,
    86
  Feta Cream, 13
  Herb Cheese, 20
  Indonesian Cream, 14
  Orange Cream Cheese, 13
  Salmon Mousse, 64
  Shrimp & Red Onion, 15
  We'll Name It Later, 25
Stuffed Cucumber Cups, 45
SUBSTITUTES
  Baking Powder, 92
  Brown Sugar, 93
  Icing Sugar, 89
  Madeira, 74
  Shallots, 41
  Vanilla, 87
Sugared Peanuts, 101
SWEETS
  Almond Butter Cake, 87
  Almond Roca Bars, 88
  Ice Cream Cookies, 89
  Lemon Cheese Fingers, 90
  Millionaire Bars, 91
  Sesame Seed Cookies, 92
  Spice Cookies, 93
Sweet & Sour Bow Ties, 58
Swiss Cheese Stacks, 14

Tangy Sweet Mustard, 83
Teriyaki Steak, 73

Terrine of Chicken, Ham &
  Sausage, 79
Terrine of Fresh Vegetables, 62
Toasted Nut & Dried Fruit
  Mix, 102
Toast Rolls, 33
Tringles, 52
Tuna & Caper Filling, 32

VEGETABLES
  Antipasto, 16
  Avocado & Salmon Filling, 27
  Celery & Olive Relish, 85
  Corned Beef & Green Pepper
    Filling, 28
  Eggplant & Olive Relish, 86
  Guacamole Sauce, 17
  Mediterranean Pastries, 44
  Mini Dogs 'n Sauerkraut, 76
  Mini Omelettes, 61
  Mushroom Tart, 41
  Mushroom Turnovers, 39
  Onion Wafers, 54
  Spinach Filling, 35
  Spinach Pâté, 60
  Spinach Tart, 42
  Stuffed Cucumber Cups, 45
  Terrine of Fresh Vegetables, 62

WAFERS
  Gruyère Shortbread, 53
  Onion, 54
  Stilton, 55
  Tringles, 52
  Whole Wheat Cheddar Hearts,
    54
We'll Name It Later Spread, 25
White Grape Punch, 99
White Sangria, 99
Whole Wheat Cheddar Hearts, 54